MICROSOFT EXCEL® 5.0 FOR WINDOWS™

Sarah E. Hutchinson
Stacey C. Sawyer
Glen J. Coulthard

THE IRWIN ADVANTAGE SERIES
FOR COMPUTER EDUCATION

IRWIN

Chicago • Bogota • Boston • Buenos Aires • Caracas
London • Madrid • Mexico City • Sydney • Toronto

ISBN 0-256-17012-6

4 5 6 7 8 9 0 ML 1 0 9 8 7 6 5

TABLE OF CONTENTS

SESSION 1: FUNDAMENTALS

SESSION 2: WORKING WITH SPREADSHEETS

SESSION 3: INCREASING YOUR PRODUCTIVITY

SESSION 4: MANAGING A WORKBOOK

SESSION 5: CREATING CHARTS

USING THIS GUIDE

This tutorial is one in a series of learning guides that lead you through the most popular microcomputer software programs available. Concepts, skills, and procedures are grouped into session topics and are presented in a logical and structured manner. Commands and procedures are introduced using hands-on examples, and you are encouraged to perform the steps along with the guide. Although you may turn directly to a later session, be aware that some sessions require, or at least assume, that you have completed the previous sessions. For maximum benefit, you should also work through the short answer questions and hands-on exercises appearing at the end of each session.

The exercises and examples in this guide use several standard conventions to indicate menu options, keystroke combinations, and command instructions.

MENU INSTRUCTIONS

In Windows, all Menu bar options and pull-down menu commands have an underlined or highlighted letter in each option. When you need to execute a command from the Menu bar—the row of menu choices across the top of the screen—the tutorial's instruction line separates the Menu bar option from the command with a comma. For example, the command for quitting Windows is shown as:

CHOOSE: File, Exit

This instruction tells you to choose the File option on the Menu bar and then to choose the Exit command from the File pull-down menu. The actual steps for choosing a menu command are discussed later in this guide.

KEYSTROKES AND KEYSTROKE COMBINATIONS

When two keys must be pressed together, the tutorial's instruction line shows the keys joined with a plus (+) sign. For example, you can execute a command from the Windows Menu bar by holding down (Alt) and then pressing the key with the underlined or highlighted letter of the desired command.

To illustrate this type of keystroke combination, the following statement shows how to access the File menu option:

PRESS: Alt+f

In this instruction, you press the Alt key first and then hold it down while you press f. Once both keys have been pressed, they are then immediately released.

COMMAND INSTRUCTIONS

This guide indicates with a special typeface data that you are required to type in yourself. For example:

TYPE: `Income Statement`

When you are required to enter unique information, such as the current date or your name, the instruction appears in italics. The following instruction directs you to type your name in place of the actual words: "your name."

TYPE: *`your name`*

Instructions that use general directions rather than a specific option or command name appear italicized in the regular typeface.

SELECT: *a different pattern for the chart*

ADVANTAGE DISKETTE

The Advantage Diskette, provided with this guide or by your instructor, contains the files that you use in each session and in the hands-on exercises. This diskette is extremely important for ensuring the success of the guide.

If you are using this guide in a self-study program, we suggest that you make a copy of the Advantage Diskette using the DOS DISKCOPY command. When the guide asks you to insert the Advantage Diskette, you insert and work with the copied diskette instead. By following this procedure, you will be able to work through the guide again at a later date using a fresh copy of the Advantage Diskette. For more information on using the DISKCOPY command, please refer to your DOS manual.

MICROSOFT EXCEL 5.0: FUNDAMENTALS

Be thankful for the electronic spreadsheet, one of the most commonly used business software tools! Just a few years ago, a spreadsheet existed only in paper form and its 7,500 or so tiny spaces had to be filled in by hand. Many a manager, accountant, and business planner wore down several pencils (and erasers) revising this paper instrument. Today, electronic spreadsheets, such as Microsoft Excel, enable you to insert and change numbers with ease. This session shows you how to begin using this valuable tool.

PREVIEW

When you have completed this session, you will be able to:

Explain the applications for electronic spreadsheets.

•

Load Windows and start Microsoft Excel.

•

Access the Help facility.

•

Move around a worksheet and a workbook.

•

Enter and edit data in a worksheet.

•

Perform the Undo command.

•

Save, close, and retrieve workbooks.

•

Exit Microsoft Excel.

1

SESSION OUTLINE

Why This Session Is Important
Working with Electronic Spreadsheets
Planning Your Spreadsheet
The Windows Advantage
Features of Microsoft Excel 5.0
Working with Microsoft Excel
     How the Mouse Is Used
     How the Keyboard Is Used
Starting Excel
The Guided Tour
     Application Window
     Document Window
     Menu Bar
     Shortcut Menus
     Dialog Box
     Toolbars
Getting Help
Moving the Cell Pointer
Overview of Data Entry
     Entering Text
     Entering Dates
     Entering Numbers
     Entering Formulas
Editing a Cell
Erasing a Cell
Using the Undo Command
Saving and Closing a Workbook
Leaving Excel
Summary
     Command Summary
Key Terms
Exercises
     Short Answer
     Hands-On

WHY THIS SESSION IS IMPORTANT

This guide leads you step-by-step through one of the most popular spreadsheet programs available, Microsoft Excel 5.0 for Windows. You will initially concentrate on spreadsheet fundamentals and then explore the basic procedures and commands required to work effectively with Excel. In this first session, you will learn about the primary components of the program and how to enter text, numbers, dates, and formulas into a worksheet. The session also includes sections on using the Help facility and Undo command. Lastly, you will learn how to save related worksheets to the disk in a single workbook file.

WORKING WITH ELECTRONIC SPREADSHEETS

The electronic spreadsheet has been available for personal computers since the introduction of VisiCalc in 1978. The arrival of Lotus 1-2-3 in 1983 launched the second generation of spreadsheet software, expanding the perceived use of the spreadsheet from a visual calculator (VisiCalc) to an all-around business tool. Microsoft Excel for Windows is helping lead the electronic spreadsheet into its third generation, adding an easy-to-use graphical interface, spreadsheet publishing capabilities, and single-step functionality.

For years, people have used calculators and long rolls of paper to perform numerical calculations. With the recent advancements in computers and electronic spreadsheets, these manual tools may soon be considered obsolete. Accountants, engineers, and business people now use spreadsheets to analyze their financial and statistical data. However, spreadsheets are much more than glorified calculators; often they are the primary tool used in business.

An electronic spreadsheet is similar to a manual worksheet or an accountant's ledger. With a manual worksheet, you write descriptive labels down the first column and then make entries under adjacent column headings (often, monthly, quarterly, or yearly headings). An electronic spreadsheet is also composed of rows and columns. You create a spreadsheet in much the same way as before, by entering information into cells, or intersections of the rows and the columns.

One of the primary advantages of an electronic spreadsheet over a manual worksheet is the ability to perform **what-if analysis**. The term *what-if* refers to your ability to change a value in the spreadsheet and immediately see the effects it has on other calculations. For example, *"What if my annual sales were only 5,000 units? How would that affect my net income?"* or *"What if the interest rate was 7.5%? How would that affect my mortgage payment?"* This capability makes the electronic spreadsheet one of the most valuable planning tools available.

Some additional advantages of using electronic spreadsheets are these:

- *Electronic spreadsheets are much larger than manual worksheets.*
  While manual worksheets are limited by paper size, electronic spreadsheets typically contain hundreds of columns and thousands of rows. This expansive area allows you to keep related information together and to produce reports that are larger than a normal page.

- *Electronic spreadsheets can perform mathematical, statistical, and financial calculations quickly and accurately.*
  The primary use of a spreadsheet is to calculate **formulas**, such as 200+350, that are entered into its cells.

- *Cells in electronic spreadsheets can use information from other cells.*
  A formula may consist solely of numbers or it may refer to other cells in the spreadsheet. Rather than entering the values 200+350, a formula can reference the cells that contain these numbers. With a manual worksheet, changing a single number can mean hours of extra work in recalculating figures. Changing a number in an electronic spreadsheet, however, immediately produces a ripple effect of recalculations for all formulas dependent upon that value.

- *Electronic spreadsheets can be stored and retrieved for repeated use.*
  You can permanently save electronic spreadsheets onto diskettes, hard disks, or other types of media for safe storage. Rather than searching through endless filing cabinets for handwritten worksheets, you can use your computer's electronic filing system to retrieve files instantaneously. An electronic spreadsheet can be retrieved, edited, updated, printed, and then saved under a new name quickly and easily.

PLANNING YOUR SPREADSHEET

Would you start building a house or an office building before receiving an architect's plans? Probably not! Even experienced builders rely heavily on the planning phase before breaking new ground. Likewise, you wouldn't want to create a spreadsheet without first having a clear objective. This section provides some guidelines to help you plan and develop your electronic spreadsheets.

Use the following steps to create a spreadsheet:

1. *Establish your objectives.*
   Ask yourself why you are creating a spreadsheet. Is it to save time on lengthy calculations or to provide a regular template for a monthly report? By clearly stating your objectives, you will gain a better understanding of the requirements of the spreadsheet.

2. *Define the output requirements.*
   Since the layout or structure of a spreadsheet is largely determined by the type of reports required, you should mock up the reports on paper before creating the spreadsheet on the computer.

3. *Construct the spreadsheet.*
   Having completed your needs assessment, you now construct the spreadsheet. Most people prefer to enter the known information first (row and column headings) and then create the formulas.

4. *Test and use the spreadsheet.*
   Testing involves performing manual calculations on various parts of the spreadsheet and then comparing those values with the spreadsheet's results. Don't take it for granted that a spreadsheet's calculations are correct—a simple typing mistake can cause numerous errors. A spreadsheet is a dynamic tool and must be updated and maintained to remain relevant.

5. *Document the spreadsheet.*
   A spreadsheet can become quite complex. Proper documentation is essential, especially when the spreadsheet is used by several different people. Documentation consists of on-screen and paper instructions specifying where and how information is to be entered and outlining the formulas used to perform calculations.

THE WINDOWS ADVANTAGE

Microsoft Excel is the best-selling spreadsheet software program for the Windows environment. With tens of millions of copies sold in the last few years, Windows is the environment of choice for personal computer users worldwide. This section explains some of the benefits of working in the Windows environment.

Microsoft Windows is a software program that works with DOS to provide a **graphical user interface** (GUI) for programs. A graphical interface makes using computers easier and more intuitive for most people. With Windows, you use a pointing device called a **mouse** to select **icons** (pictures that represent programs or functions).

Some of the advantages of working in the Windows environment include these features:

- *Windows programs are easy to learn and use.*
  Windows provides a standardized interface for all programs, whether they are word processing, spreadsheet, or database applications. As a result, you can use the knowledge acquired from one Windows product in working with other Windows products.

- *The ability to run more than one application at a time.*
  Windows is a **multitasking** environment whereby more than one application or program may be running at the same time. For example, multitasking allows you to simultaneously receive an electronic mail message, calculate an Excel spreadsheet, and print a report.

- *The ability to exchange information among applications.*
  Windows provides a program called Clipboard that lets you copy and move information within an application or among applications. For example, it's easy to copy a budget from an Excel spreadsheet to the Clipboard and then paste that budget into a Word document.

- *The ability to display on the screen what you will get from the printer.*
  This feature is called **WYSIWYG** ("What You See Is What You Get"); it allows different fonts, borders, and graphics to be displayed on the screen at all times.

FEATURES OF MICROSOFT EXCEL 5.0

At the time of this writing, the latest release of Microsoft Excel for Windows is version 5.0. To ensure its competitiveness in the marketplace, Microsoft introduced several significant features in Excel 5.0. This section highlights some of these enhancements.

- Excel 5.0 files are now called *workbooks*. Each workbook may contain worksheets, chart sheets, macro sheets, and Visual Basic programming modules. The number of worksheets you can create in a workbook is limited only by the memory within your computer.

- Excel 5.0 lets you access context-sensitive commands on a pop-up or shortcut menu by pointing at an item, such as a cell or chart, with the mouse pointer and clicking the right mouse button.

- Excel 5.0 provides custom toolbars for single-step mouse access to formatting, drawing, charting, and other menu commands. You can display more than one toolbar at a time and hide, move, and customize toolbars as required.

- Excel 5.0 provides new wizards that simplify the process of creating crosstab tables (not discussed in this guide), entering functions, and importing text. The new TipWizard even watches your keystrokes while you work, offering helpful shortcuts and other suggestions.

- Excel 5.0 incorporates many features from Word 6.0, including a fully integrated spelling checker, file search utility, and a summary dialog box for collecting additional information about a workbook file.

- Excel 5.0 still includes the popular AutoFill and AutoFormat commands. The AutoFill feature lets you create a series, such as a range of dates, by dragging the mouse over the worksheet. The AutoFormat feature lets you apply a predefined table format to a worksheet area, complete with fonts, borders, colors, and shading.

If you are new to electronic spreadsheet programs, you may not understand all of the terms used in the above discussion. Don't despair—you'll definitely understand the importance and utility of these features by the end of this guide. Now, let's begin our journey through Microsoft Excel 5.0.

WORKING WITH MICROSOFT EXCEL

Microsoft Excel 5.0 is a complex yet easy-to-learn program. As you proceed through this guide, you will find that there are often three methods for performing the same command or procedure in Excel:

- Menu   Select a command or procedure from the Menu bar.

- Mouse   Point to and click a toolbar button.

- Keyboard   Press a keyboard shortcut (usually $\boxed{\text{Ctrl}}$+*a letter*).

Although this guide concentrates on the quickest and easiest methods, we recommend that you try the others and decide which you prefer. *Don't memorize all of the methods and information in this guide! Be selective.*

HOW THE MOUSE IS USED

You may use Excel with only a keyboard but much of the program's basic design revolves around the availability of a mouse. Regardless of whether your mouse has two or three buttons, you use the left or primary mouse button for selecting workbook items and menu commands and the right or secondary mouse button for displaying shortcut menus.

The most common mouse actions used in Excel are these:

- Point   Slide the mouse on your desk to position the tip of the mouse pointer over the object on the screen.

- Click   Press down and release the left mouse button quickly. Clicking is used to select a cell in the worksheet and to choose menu commands.

- Right-Click   Press down and release the right mouse button. Right-clicking the mouse pointer on an object displays a context-sensitive shortcut menu.

- Double-Click   Press down and release the mouse button twice in rapid succession. Double-clicking is used to perform in-cell editing and to modify the tab names.

- Drag   Press down and hold the mouse button as you move the mouse pointer across the screen. When the mouse pointer reaches the desired location, release the mouse button. Dragging is used to select a group of cells and to copy or move data.

You may notice that the mouse pointer changes shape as you move it over different parts of the screen. Each mouse pointer shape has its own purpose and may provide you with important information. There are four primary mouse shapes that appear in Excel:

↖	arrow	Used to choose menu commands, access the toolbars, and complete dialog boxes.
✛	cross	Used to select cells and groups of cells in a worksheet.
⧗	hourglass	Informs you that Excel is occupied with another task and requests that you wait.
I	I-beam	Used to modify and edit text in the Formula bar and in a cell.

As you proceed through this guide, other mouse shapes will be explained in the appropriate sections.

HOW THE KEYBOARD IS USED

Aside from being the primary input device for creating a worksheet, the keyboard offers shortcut methods for performing commands and procedures. For example, several menu commands have shortcut key combinations listed to the right of the command in the pull-down menu. Therefore, you can perform a command by simply pressing the shortcut keys rather than accessing the Menu bar. Many of these shortcut key combinations are available throughout Windows applications.

STARTING EXCEL

This session assumes that you are working on a computer with DOS, Windows, and Microsoft Excel 5.0 loaded on the hard disk drive. Before you can use Excel, you must turn on the computer and load Microsoft Windows into the computer's memory. Perform the following steps on your computer.

1. Turn on the power switches to the computer and monitor. The C:\> prompt or a menu appears, announcing that your computer has successfully loaded the Disk Operating System (DOS). (*Note*: Your computer may automatically load Microsoft Windows when it is first turned on. If this is the case, you can skip to step 3.)

2. To start Microsoft Windows from the C:\> prompt:
   TYPE: win
   PRESS: (Enter)
   After a few seconds, the Windows logo appears on the screen followed by the **Program Manager** window (Figure 1.1). (*Note*: The icons on your Program Manager screen may not be exactly the same as Figure 1.1; icons represent the programs that are stored on your hard disk.)

Figure 1.1

The Microsoft Windows Program Manager window

Program Manager Window

Microsoft Office Group Icon

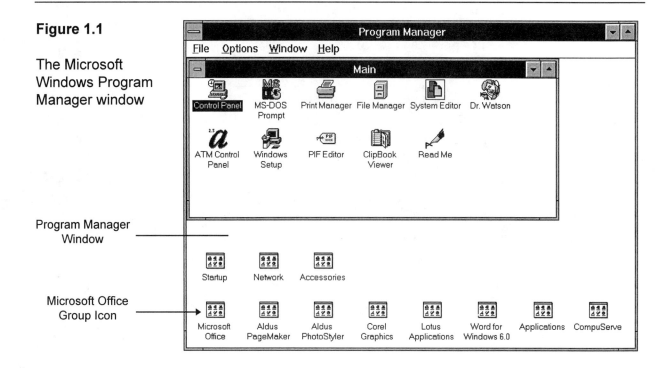

3. The Microsoft Excel 5.0 program is often located in a group window called either Microsoft Excel 5.0 or Microsoft Office (the Microsoft Office icon is shown in Figure 1.1.) To open a group window, you double-click its group icon. If you see the Microsoft Office group icon in your Program Manager, double-click it to display a group window similar to the following:

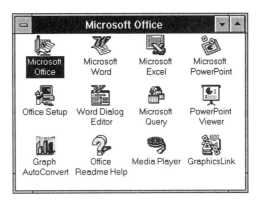

If you see a Microsoft Excel group icon, double-click the icon to display its group window. (*Note*: During the installation of Excel to your hard disk, you specify the group window where Excel will appear. Therefore, you may have a group window for Excel different from what appears in the Figures and instructions in this guide.)

4. To load Excel from the group window:
DOUBLE-CLICK: Microsoft Excel program icon (⬛)

Quick Reference *Loading Microsoft Excel 5.0*	1. DOUBLE-CLICK: Microsoft Excel group icon (or Microsoft Office group icon)
	2. DOUBLE-CLICK: Microsoft Excel program icon

THE GUIDED TOUR

Software programs designed for Microsoft Windows, such as Excel, Word, and PageMaker, have many similarities in screen design and layout. Each program operates in its own application window, while spreadsheets, letters, and brochures are created in separate document windows. This section explores the various parts of Excel, including the tools for manipulating application and document windows.

APPLICATION WINDOW

When you first load Excel, the screen displays the **application window** and a maximized **document window**. The application window (Figure 1.2) contains the Title bar, Menu bar, Standard toolbar, Formatting toolbar, Formula bar and Name box, and Status bar. You create new worksheets or open existing worksheets in the document area. In Figure 1.2, the document area is covered by a maximized document window.

Figure 1.2

Application window

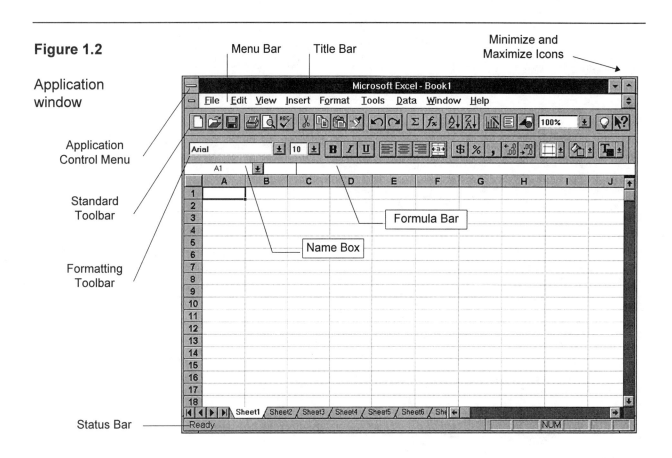

The primary components of the application window are:

Application Control menu (⊟)	Used to size and position the application window using the keyboard. To quit Excel, you can double-click the Application Control menu.

Minimize (▾) and Maximize (▴) or Restore (↕) icons	Located in the top right-hand corner of the Application window, these triangular-shaped icons are used to control the display of the application window using the mouse.
Title bar	The Title bar contains the name of the program or data file. Using a mouse, you can move a window by dragging its Title bar.
Menu bar	Contains the Excel menu commands.
Standard toolbar	Displays buttons for opening and saving workbooks, copying and moving information, and accessing special features using a mouse.
Formatting toolbar	Displays buttons for accessing character and cell formatting commands using the mouse.
Formula bar	The Formula bar appears below the Toolbars and includes the Name box, which shows your current location on the worksheet.
Status bar	Located at the bottom of the application window, the Status bar displays information about key toggle status and other helpful information.

You can size, move, and manipulate the Excel application window on the Windows desktop to customize your work environment.

DOCUMENT WINDOW

You create and store your worksheets, charts, and macros in a special file called a **workbook**. You can think of an Excel workbook as a three-ring binder with tabs at the beginning of each new section or topic. In a workbook, you can add and delete sheets, copy information from one sheet to another, and organize your information into logical sections. Each workbook appears in its own document window which can be minimized, maximized, or displayed as a window.

A worksheet (Figure 1.3) is the most common sheet that you create in an Excel workbook file. Each new workbook contains 16 blank worksheets labeled Sheet1, Sheet2, and so on to Sheet16. Similar to a large piece of ledger paper, a worksheet is divided into vertical columns and horizontal rows. The 16,384 rows are numbered and the 256 columns are labeled from A to Z, then AA to AZ, and so on to column IV. The intersection of a column and a row is called a **cell**. Each cell is given a **cell address** consisting of its column letter followed by its row number (for example, B4 or AX400).

Figure 1.3

Document window

Document Control Menu

Cell

Tab Scrolling Arrows

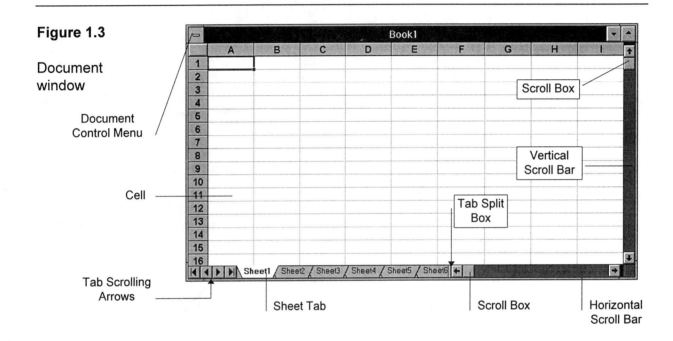

Sheet Tab

Scroll Box

Horizontal Scroll Bar

A document window consists of the following parts:

Document Control menu (⊐)	Used to size and position the window using the keyboard. To close a worksheet, you can double-click the Document Control menu.
Scroll bars	Placed at the right and bottom borders of the document window, scroll bars facilitate moving around a worksheet using the mouse.
Sheet tabs	Sheet tabs identify the various pages in a workbook. Using the mouse, you click a tab to move to that particular page or double-click a tab to rename it.

Tab Split box	Using the mouse, you drag the tab split box to increase and decrease the space shared by the sheet tabs and the horizontal scroll bar.
Tab Scrolling arrows	Using the mouse, you click the tab scrolling arrows to move quickly to the first sheet, previous sheet, next sheet, or last sheet in a workbook file.

You should recognize some familiar components in the document window that appear in all windows. For example, the Minimize and Maximize icons appear in the top right-hand corner of the document window. To restore a maximized document to a window, you click the Restore icon (↕). To maximize the document window, you click the Maximize icon (▲). Before proceeding, make sure that your document window is maximized.

You can display several workbook files concurrently within the Excel application window. For example, you may want to view the spreadsheet results from various departments on the screen at the same time. Assuming that the departmental data is divided into separate workbooks, you can open each file in its own document window. Another method for accomplishing this type of summary view is to create and store multiple worksheets in a single workbook. Similar to peeling off pages from a notepad, you enter each department's data on its own worksheet and then consolidate the data in a summary sheet. In Session 4, you learn how to work with multiple workbook files and multiple-sheet workbooks.

MENU BAR

Excel commands are grouped together on the Menu bar, as shown below.

Commands in this guide are written in the following form: *Edit, Copy*, where *Edit* is the Menu bar option and *Copy* is the command to be selected from the pull-down menu. To execute a command using the mouse, click once on the Menu bar option and then click once on the pull-down menu command. Using the keyboard, you hold down the (Alt) key and tap the underlined letter of the desired option on the Menu bar. When the pull-down menu is displayed, press the underlined letter of the command you want to execute. Commands that are not available for selection appear dimmed. Commands that are followed by an ellipsis (...) require further information to be collected in a dialog box.

SHORTCUT MENUS

Excel provides context-sensitive shortcut menus for quick access to menu commands. Rather than searching for commands in the Menu bar, you position the mouse pointer on an object, such as a worksheet cell, and click the right mouse button. A pop-up menu appears with the most commonly selected commands for the object.

To practice accessing the Menu bar and shortcut menus, perform the following steps on your computer.

1. To choose the Help command, position the tip of the mouse pointer on the word Help in the Menu bar and click the left mouse button once. A pull-down menu appears below the Help option.

2. To display a pull-down menu for the File option:
    CHOOSE: File
    This instruction tells you to click the mouse pointer on File in the Menu bar. (*Note*: All menu commands that you execute in this guide begin with the word "CHOOSE.")

3. To leave the Menu bar without making a selection:
    CHOOSE: File
    (*Note*: Clicking the menu option again removes the pull-down menu. You can also click anywhere on the screen, away from the pull-down menu, to remove a menu.)

4. To display a shortcut or pop-up menu, position the mouse pointer over any button on the Standard toolbar and click the right mouse button. The shortcut menu at the right should appear.

√ Standard
√ Formatting
Chart
Drawing
Forms
Visual Basic
Auditing
WorkGroup
Microsoft
Toolbars...
Customize...

5. To remove the shortcut menu from the screen, move the mouse pointer away from the menu and click the right mouse button a second time. The shortcut menu disappears.

Quick Reference *Using Shortcut* *Menus*	1. Position the mouse pointer over an item, such as a toolbar button. 2. CLICK: the right mouse button to display a shortcut or pop-up menu 3. CHOOSE: *a command from the menu*, or CLICK: the right mouse button away from the menu to remove it

DIALOG BOX

Excel uses dialog boxes (Figure 1.4) to collect information necessary to execute a command. An ellipsis (...) following a command on a pull-down or pop-up menu informs you that Excel will present a dialog box when the command is selected. Dialog boxes are also used to display messages or ask for confirmation of commands.

Figure 1.4

Example of a dialog box

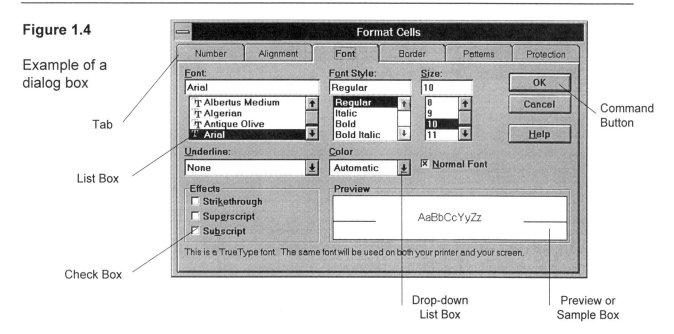

A dialog box uses several methods for collecting information, as shown in Figure 1.4 above and described in Table 1.1 below.

Table 1.1	*Component*	*Description*
Parts of a dialog box	Tabs	A new feature in Excel 5.0: dialog boxes with tabs allow you to access other pages of options by simply clicking on a named tab at the top of the window.
	List box	A scrollable list of choices. Use the scroll bars or arrow keys to browse the list.
	Text box	A box for collecting typed information. Before typing your entry you must click in the text box to select it.
	Drop-down list	A list of available choices in which only one item is displayed at a time. Using a mouse, click on the adjacent arrow to display the full list of choices. To select an item, use the scroll bars to move through the list and then click the desired item.
	Check box	An option that can be turned on or off. Click the mouse pointer in the box to toggle the × mark on and off. The option is turned on when an × appears.
	Option button	One option that can be selected from a group of related options. Click the mouse pointer on the desired option button to select it.
	Command button	A button that executes an action when selected. Most dialog boxes provide the Help button to offer quick access to a help screen explaining the items in the dialog box.

TOOLBARS

Assuming that you haven't yet customized your Excel screen, you will see the Standard and Formatting toolbars appear below the Menu bar. Excel provides a wide variety of toolbars and buttons for quick and easy mouse access to its more popular commands and features. Don't worry about memorizing the button names appearing in the following graphics—the majority of these buttons are explained in subsequent sessions. You can also point at any toolbar button and pause until a yellow ToolTip appears with the button name.

The Standard toolbar (Figure 1.5) provides access to file management and editing commands in addition to special features like the Function Wizard and the ChartWizard:

Figure 1.5

Standard toolbar

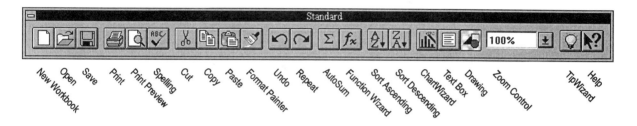

The Formatting toolbar (Figure 1.6) lets you access character and cell formatting commands:

Figure 1.6

Formatting toolbar

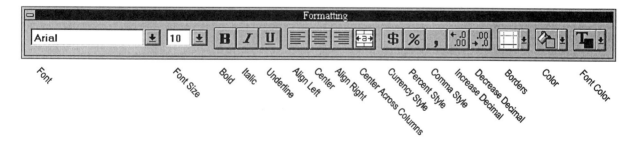

To practice displaying and hiding toolbars, perform the following steps on your computer.

1. Position the mouse pointer over any button on the Standard toolbar.

2. CLICK: right mouse button to display the shortcut menu

3. To display the Drawing toolbar:
    CHOOSE: Drawing
    The new toolbar appears, usually in its own window as shown below:

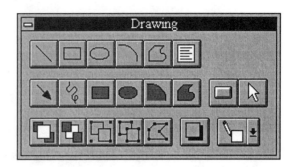

4. If the Drawing toolbar appears in a window as above, move to step 5. If, on the other hand, the Drawing toolbar appears "docked" against a border of the application window, you must drag it away from the border to make it a free-floating window. To un-dock a toolbar, position the mouse pointer on any part of the toolbar that is not a button or drop-down list. Once positioned, click the left mouse button and hold it down and then drag the toolbar to the center of the application window. The toolbar turns into a window, complete with a Title bar and Control menu.

5. To move the Drawing toolbar:
    DRAG: Drawing toolbar's Title bar around the application window
    This instruction tells you to position the mouse pointer over the toolbar's Title bar, click the mouse button and hold it down, and then move the mouse pointer to move the window.

6. To remove the Drawing toolbar:
    CLICK: Drawing toolbar's Control menu once
    The Drawing toolbar disappears from the application window.

GETTING HELP

Similar to most software programs, Excel provides context-sensitive Help when you press the F1 key. *Context-sensitive* refers to Word's ability to retrieve Help information reflecting your current position in the program. For example, you can highlight a menu option and press F1 to display a

Help window containing a description of the command. Perhaps an easier method for accessing Help for menu commands is to click the Help button (?) on the Standard toolbar and then select the desired command using the question mark mouse pointer. Rather than executing the command, Excel displays its Help window.

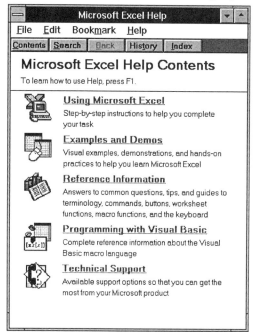

To access the table of contents for Excel's Help facility, choose the Help, Contents command from the menu. The resulting Help window is shown at the right. You can browse the contents by clicking on words and phrases that are green and have a solid underline. These are called **jump terms** because they allow you to jump quickly to topics of interest. Words or phrases that are green and have a dotted underline provide definition boxes when they are clicked. To remove the definition, you simply click the box.

If you have access to a computer for practice, you may want to peruse the Excel 5.0 Quick Preview. To start this tour of Excel's features, you choose Help, Quick Preview from the menu. To return to Excel, you click the Return to Microsoft Excel command button on the main screen (shown below in Figure 1.7).

Figure 1.7

Excel's Quick
Preview

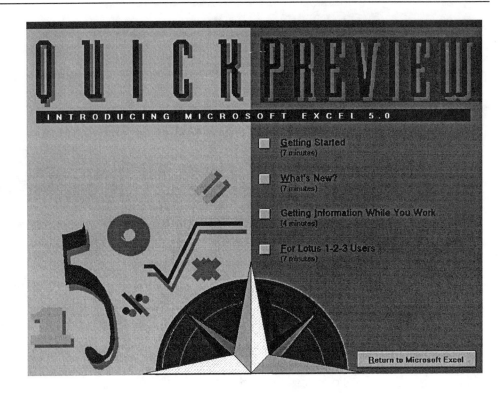

The best way to learn about Excel's Help facility is to practice using it.
Perform the following steps.

1. In the next several steps, you'll access Help for the File, New
   command, the File, Print command, and one of the toolbar buttons.
   Let's start with the File, New command. Position the tip of the mouse
   pointer over the Help button (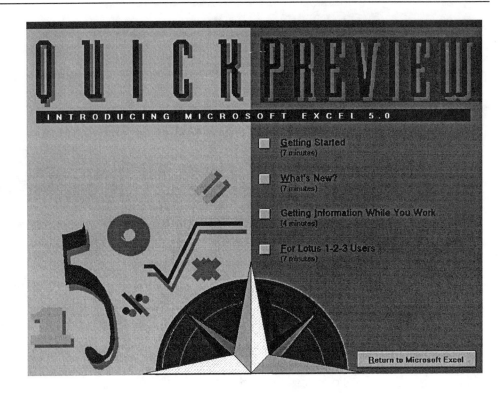) on the Standard toolbar.

2. To activate the question mark mouse pointer:
   CLICK: Help button () once

3. CHOOSE: File, New
   Rather than executing the command, Excel retrieves a Help window.

4. Read the contents of the Help window. Once finished, you close the
   window by executing the following command from its Menu bar:
   CHOOSE: File, Exit
   (*Note:* You can also close a Help window by double-clicking its
   Control menu.)

5. To access Help for the Save button () on the Standard toolbar:
   CLICK: Help button () to get the question mark mouse pointer

6. CLICK: Save button (⊟)
   A Help window appears describing the Save command.

7. To close the Help window:
   DOUBLE-CLICK: Control menu (⚊) for the Help window
   (*Caution:* Ensure that you are clicking the Help window's Control menu and not Excel's Control menu.)

8. To search for Help on a specific topic or command (for example, printing), do the following:
   DOUBLE-CLICK: Help button (▶?)
   The Help window appears followed by the Search dialog box. Make sure that the dialog box is displayed before continuing to the next step.

9. TYPE: print
   The list box automatically scrolls to the first occurrence of "print."

10. SELECT: Print command (File menu) option
    SELECT: Show Topics command button
    In this instruction, the word SELECT means to click the command button with the mouse.

11. SELECT: Print command (File menu) option in the bottom window
    SELECT: Go To command button

12. Read the contents of the resulting Help window and then close it using either method described above.

13. Excel also provides a special Help tool called the TipWizard. The TipWizard watches your keystrokes as you work and offers suggestions and shortcuts. To start the TipWizard:
    CLICK: TipWizard button (💡) on the Standard toolbar
    A tips box appears beneath the Formatting toolbar.

14. To remove the TipWizard box:
    CLICK: TipWizard button (💡) on the Standard toolbar

Quick Reference *Using Help*	• PRESS: F1, or • CLICK: Help button (▶?), or • CHOOSE: Help, Contents

MOVING THE CELL POINTER

When you first open a new workbook, the **cell pointer** is positioned on cell A1 in Sheet1. For your convenience, Excel displays the current cell address in the Name box at the left-hand side of the Formula bar. In this section, you learn how to move the cell pointer around the worksheet using the mouse and keyboard. Although rudimentary, these skills are vital for efficiently creating and viewing worksheets.

Perform the following steps, starting at cell A1.

1. To move the cell pointer to cell G4 using the keyboard:
    PRESS: [→] six times
    PRESS: [↓] three times
    Notice that the cell address appears in the Name box.

2. To move to cell E12 using a mouse:
    CLICK: cell E12
    (*Hint*: Position the cross mouse pointer over cell E12 and click the left mouse button once.)

3. To move to cell E24 using the keyboard:
    PRESS: [↓] 12 times
    You may notice that the first few rows scroll off the top of the screen.

4. To move to cell E124 using the keyboard, there is an easier method than pressing the [↓] key 100 times. The [PgUp] and [PgDn] keys are used to move up and down a worksheet by as many rows as fit in the current document window. In other words, if the document window displays 15 rows of your worksheet, pressing [PgDn] will move you down 15 rows at a time. To move to cell E124, do the following:
    PRESS: [PgDn] until cell E124 is in view
    PRESS: arrow keys to move to cell E124

5. To move back to cell E24 using the mouse:
    CLICK: on the vertical scroll bar, above the scroll box (▦), repeatedly
    CLICK: cell E24 to move the cell pointer
    You can also drag the scroll box (▦) or click the up scroll arrow (▣) on the vertical scroll bar.

6. To move to cell AE24:
    CLICK: on the horizontal scroll bar, to the right of the scroll box (▨),
    repeatedly
    CLICK: cell AE24 to move the cell pointer

7. To move back to cell E24:
    DRAG: scroll box (▨) to the left on the horizontal scroll bar
    CLICK: cell E24 to move the cell pointer

8. To move to the first cell (A1) in the worksheet using the keyboard:
    PRESS: Ctrl + Home
    With a mouse, use the vertical and horizontal scroll bars. When cell A1
    is in view, position the mouse pointer over the cell and click once.

9. To move the cell pointer in any direction until the cell contents change
    from empty to filled, filled to empty, or until a border is encountered,
    press Ctrl with an arrow key. To move to cell IV16384 (the last cell
    in the bottom right-hand corner of the worksheet):
    PRESS: Ctrl + →
    PRESS: Ctrl + ↓

10. You can use the Name box to move directly to any cell in the
    worksheet. To move to cell AA100, for example:
    CLICK: Name box
    The cell address in the Name box will appear highlighted.

11. TYPE: aa100
    PRESS: Enter
    You are taken immediately to cell AA100.

12. To move back to cell A1:
    PRESS: Ctrl + Home

OVERVIEW OF DATA ENTRY

You create a worksheet by entering information into the individual cells.
A worksheet can be as simple as a five-item household budget or as
complex as an order entry and invoicing application. The remainder of this
session explores the basic building blocks for creating a worksheet using
Excel, including entering, editing, and deleting cell information.

There are several types of information that may be entered into a worksheet cell: text, numbers, dates and times, formulas, and functions. Regardless of the type of information, you enter data by moving the cell pointer to a cell and then typing what you want to place into the cell. The information that you type appears in Excel's Formula bar. To transfer the information from the Formula bar into the cell, you press (Enter) or an arrow key. You can also click on another cell using the mouse.

To practice entering information, you will create the worksheet appearing in Figure 1.8 by the completion of this section.

Figure 1.8

Sample worksheet

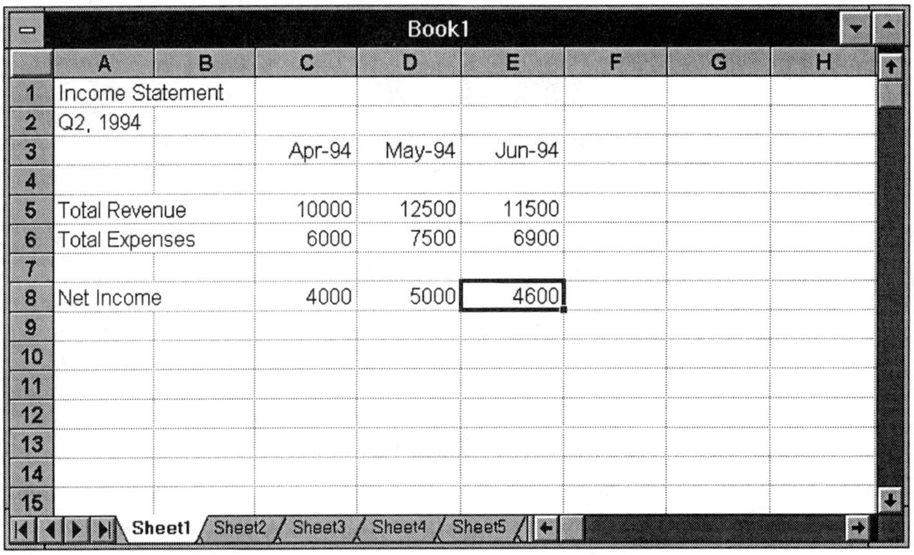

ENTERING TEXT

Text labels enhance the readability of a worksheet with headings, instructions, and descriptive information. Although a typical worksheet column is only eight or nine characters wide, a single cell in a worksheet can hold hundreds of characters. With longer entries, the text spills over into the next cell, if it is empty. Later, you will learn how to emphasize important text using different fonts and alignment options.

To begin creating the worksheet, perform the following steps.

1. Move to cell A1. (*Hint*: (Ctrl)+(Home))
   For the remainder of this guide, you can use either the keyboard or mouse to move the cell pointer.

2. As you type the following text, watch the Formula bar. Enter the following heading for the worksheet:
    TYPE: Income Statement
    Notice that there is an ☒ and a ☑ to the left of the text in the Formula bar. Rather than pressing (Enter) to accept the entry or (Esc) to cancel the entry, you can click the ☑ and ☒ symbols respectively.

3. To accept the entry:
    PRESS: (Enter)
    Notice that the words do not fit in a single cell and must spill over into column B. This is acceptable as long as you do not want to place any information into cell B1. Otherwise, you would have to increase the width of column A. Session 2 discusses changing a column's width.

    (*Note*: Excel 5.0 can automatically move the cell pointer down to the next row when you press (Enter). For the exercises in this guide, we assume that you have this feature selected. If your cell pointer did not move to A2 when you pressed (Enter), choose the Tools, Options command from the menu and select the Edit tab. From the resulting dialog box page, make sure that an × appears in the *Move Selection after Enter* check box.)

4. Move the cell pointer into the following cells and type in the corresponding text. When you are finished typing a label, you press (Enter) or a cursor-movement key to deposit it from the Formula bar to the active cell. Using the mouse, you click on the next cell after you have finished typing the label. If you make a mistake while typing, press the (BackSpace) key to delete the mistake, type the correct information, and then press (Enter).

    Enter the following text:

Move to Cell	*TYPE:*
A2	Q2, 1994
A5	Total Revenue
A6	Total Expenses
A8	Net Income

All the text data has now been entered into the worksheet.

ENTERING DATES

You enter dates as values in order to perform date arithmetic, such as calculating how many days have elapsed between two dates. Dates are typically entered into cells using the following formats: mm/dd/yy (for example, 12/31/94) or dd-mmm-yy (for example, 31-Dec-94). If you need to display monthly headings across the top of a column, you can enter a date as mmm-yy (for example, Dec-94). Although dates can be displayed in a variety of formats, Excel stores each date internally as the number of days elapsing since January 1, 1900.

Perform the following steps to enter dates into the worksheet.

1. Move to cell C3.

2. TYPE: Apr-94
    PRESS: ⟶

3. Move the cell pointer into the following cells and type in the corresponding dates:

Move to Cell	*TYPE:*
D3	May-94
E3	Jun-94

    With the cell pointer positioned on cell E3, you will notice that the Formula bar contains 6/1/1994. This is one example of the difference between the appearance of a cell and its actual contents. You will encounter other examples later in this session.

All the dates have now been entered into the worksheet.

ENTERING NUMBERS

Numbers are entered into the worksheet for use in formulas and reports. Whereas text is initially left-aligned with the cell border, numbers and dates are right-aligned. When the cell pointer is positioned on a cell that contains a number, the raw form of the number usually appears in the Formula bar. In other words, the cell may read 8.50% in the worksheet but the value in the Formula bar reads .085. Phone numbers, Social Security numbers, and Zip codes are not considered numeric values, since they are never used in mathematical calculations.

Perform the following steps.

1. Move to cell C5.

2. TYPE: `10000`
   PRESS: ⟶

3. Move the cell pointer into the following cells and type in the corresponding numbers:

Move to Cell	*TYPE:*
D5	`12,500`
E5	`11,500`

All the numeric data has now been entered into the worksheet. You are ready to enter formulas to calculate the remaining values.

Quick Reference *Entering Data*	1. Move the cell pointer to the desired cell location. 2. Type the information into the Formula bar. If you make a typing or spelling mistake, press the `BackSpace` key to erase the mistake. 3. To deposit the information into the cell, press `Enter` or an arrow key, or select a new cell using the mouse

ENTERING FORMULAS

A formula is a mathematical calculation that may contain numbers, cell references, and mathematical operators. The basic mathematical operators and rules of precedence apply to an Excel formula. These operators are similar to those found in most electronic spreadsheets (and high school algebra textbooks). For example, in the formula *(3+4)*5*, the *3+4* operation is performed before multiplying the sum by *5* because it appears in parentheses. Table 1.2 lists the common mathematical operators. As for the rules of precedence, Excel calculates what appears in parentheses first, multiplication and division operations (from left to right) second, and, lastly, addition and subtraction (again from left to right).

Table 1.2	*Symbol*	*Description*
Basic Mathematical Operators	( )	Parentheses
	*	Multiplication
	/	Division
	+	Addition
	-	Subtraction
Additional Operators	%	Percentage
	^	Exponentiation

You enter a formula into the worksheet by positioning the cell pointer where you want the result to appear and then preceding the expression with an equal sign (=). The expression itself can be entered either by typing the equation or by using a method called *pointing*. With pointing, you use the keyboard or mouse to point to or select cell addresses while constructing the formula.

In this exercise, you enter a formula that calculates Total Expenses as 60% of Total Revenue. Your first step is to move the cell pointer to where you want the result to appear and then enter the formula into the cell.

Perform the following steps.

1. Move to cell C6.

2. TYPE: =c5*60%
    PRESS: →

3. Move the cell pointer into the following cells and type in the corresponding formulas.

Move to Cell	*TYPE:*
D6	=d5*60%
E6	=e5*60%

4. Let's create a second formula to subtract Total Expenses from Total Revenue, yielding Net Income. When constructing the formula, glance at the Formula bar to see the results of your mouse clicks and keystrokes. To begin:
    SELECT: cell C8

5. In this step, you build a formula by pointing using the mouse:
    TYPE: =
    CLICK: cell C5
    TYPE: –
    CLICK: cell C6
    CLICK: ☑ in the Formula bar

6. Repeat the process for cells D8 and E8. Your worksheet should now appear similar to Figure 1.8.

Quick Reference	1.	Select the cell to contain the formula.
Entering a Formula	2.	TYPE: = (an equal sign)
	3.	Enter the desired expression (for example, A4+B4) by typing or by pointing to the cells using the mouse.
	4.	PRESS: (Enter) or CLICK: ☑ in the Formula bar

EDITING A CELL

What if you type a label, a number, or a formula into a cell and then decide it needs to be changed? Novices and experts alike make data entry errors when creating a worksheet. Fortunately, Excel provides several options for editing information that has already been entered.

The primary methods for editing information are these:

•   Before you press (Enter) or click on another cell to deposit an entry, you can correct a typing or spelling mistake using (BackSpace).

•   You can replace a cell's contents by selecting the cell and typing a new entry. When you press (Enter) or click on another cell, the new information replaces the original cell's contents.

•   If a cell's entry is too long or complicated to re-type, you can edit the entry by double-clicking the cell or by selecting the cell and pressing (F2). A flashing vertical bar appears in the cell, advising you that the entry may be modified. After making the necessary changes, you press (Enter) to overwrite the original cell or (Esc) to abort the modifications.

•   You can also move the mouse pointer into the Formula bar area until it changes into an I-beam. At this point, click the left mouse button once to begin editing the contents of the Formula bar. Clicking ☑ performs the same function as pressing (Enter) and clicking ☒ performs the same function as pressing (Esc).

Practice editing information in the worksheet.

1. SELECT: cell A1

2. TYPE: Profit/Loss Report
    PRESS: (Enter)

3. To modify the entry in cell A2 to read Quarter 2 instead of Q2:
    DOUBLE-CLICK: cell A2

4. Position the I-beam mouse pointer between the Q and the 2 and click the left mouse button once to place the insertion point.

5. TYPE: uarter
    PRESS: Space bar
    PRESS: (Enter)

6. DOUBLE-CLICK: cell A5

7. To change the work Revenue to Sales, position the I-beam mouse pointer to the left of the letter "R" in Revenue.

8. DRAG: mouse to the right until the word "Revenue" is highlighted

9. Release the left mouse button.

10. TYPE: Sales
    PRESS: (Enter) or CLICK: ☑
    Notice that the word "Revenue" is replaced with "Sales."

Quick Reference   1. DOUBLE-CLICK: the cell that you want to edit or PRESS: (F2)
Editing a Cell's   2. Use the mouse and arrow keys to edit the entry.
Contents   3. PRESS: (Enter) or CLICK: ☑

ERASING A CELL

Excel allows you to quickly erase a single cell, a group of cells, or the entire worksheet with a few simple keystrokes. To erase a cell's contents, highlight the cell and press the (Delete) key. If you would like to delete only the formatting of a cell, you choose Edit, Clear from the Menu bar to display further commands (listed in Table 1.3) on a cascading menu.

Table 1.3	*Command*	*Description*
Edit, Clear Commands	All	Removes the cell contents, formatting (for example, boldface and italics), and notes (reminders that can be attached to a cell that do not appear when printed).
	Formats	Removes the cell formatting only, leaving the contents and attached cell notes intact.
	Contents	Removes the cell contents only, leaving the formatting and attached cell notes intact; same as (Delete).
	Notes	Removes the cell notes only, leaving the cell contents and formatting intact.

In the next exercise, you practice erasing information from the worksheet.

1. Move to cell A2.

2. PRESS: (Delete) to remove the information from the cell

3. Move to cell A8.

4. CHOOSE: Edit, Clear
   CHOOSE: All from the cascading menu
   Do not perform another command until proceeding to the next section, where you learn how to undo a command.

Quick Reference	1. SELECT: the cell that you want to erase
Erasing a Cell	2. PRESS: (Delete)

USING THE UNDO COMMAND

The **Undo command** allows you to cancel the last command you performed in the worksheet. There are three methods for executing the Undo command. You can choose Edit, Undo from the menu, press the keyboard shortcut of Ctrl+z, or click the Undo button (⟲) on the Standard toolbar. Let's practice two of these methods in the next exercise.

Perform the following steps.

1. To undo the last command that you executed in the previous section:
    CLICK: Undo button (⟲)
    The words "Net Income" reappear in the worksheet.

2. SELECT: cell A1

3. PRESS: Delete

4. To undo the command executed in the last step:
    PRESS: Ctrl+z
    The title should reappear on the worksheet.

Quick Reference	• CHOOSE: Edit, Undo, or
Undo a Command	• PRESS: Ctrl+z, or
	• CLICK: Undo button (⟲) on the Standard toolbar

SAVING AND CLOSING A WORKBOOK

When you are creating a workbook, it exists only in the computer's RAM (random access memory), which is highly volatile. To permanently store your work, you must save the workbook to the hard disk or to a floppy diskette. Saving your work to a disk is similar to placing it into a filing cabinet. For important workbooks (ones that you cannot risk losing), you should save your work every 15 minutes, or whenever you're interrupted, to protect against an unexpected power outage or other catastrophe.

To save a workbook to a disk, you click the Save button (⊞) or you select the File, Save command from the menu. If you haven't saved the workbook before, a dialog box appears and you must type in a file name of up to eight characters with no spaces. When you are finished typing, press (**Enter**) or click the OK command button.

Perform the following steps to save the current workbook.

1. Make sure that the Advantage Diskette is placed into the drive.

2. CLICK: Save button (⊞)
   Excel displays a dialog box similar to the one shown in Figure 1.9; the file names and directories may differ from your dialog box.

Figure 1.9

Save As
dialog box

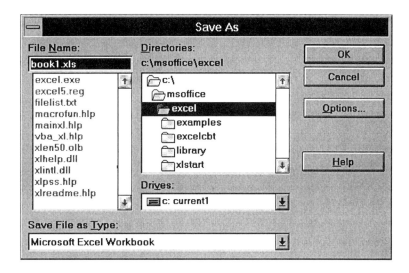

3. To specify a file name for the workbook:
   TYPE: mywork

4. To specify that the workbook be saved onto the Advantage Diskette:
   CLICK: down arrow adjacent to the Drives drop-down list box
   SELECT: a:
   If your Advantage Diskette is located in drive B:, select b: in this step.
   (*Note:* In addition to the drive, you can select a specific folder location for your file in the Directories list box. The Advantage Diskette has no folders, unlike the example in the dialog box displayed above.)

5. To proceed with saving the workbook:
   PRESS: (Enter) or CLICK: OK
   If Excel's Summary Info feature is turned on, a dialog box similar to the one shown in Figure 1.10 may appear. The information that you enter into this dialog box is useful for locating files using Excel's advanced search capabilities.

Figure 1.10

Summary Info
dialog box

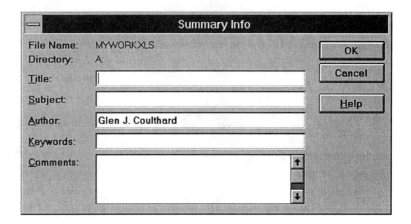

6. If the Summary Info dialog box appears, accept its contents:
   PRESS: (Enter) or CLICK: OK
   You may hear a noise from the computer's diskette drive as the file is being saved to the Advantage Diskette.

7. When you are finished working with a workbook, you should close the file to free up valuable RAM. To close the MYWORK workbook:
   CHOOSE: File, Close
   The MYWORK workbook disappears.

8. To open a new workbook:
   CLICK: New Workbook button (□)
   (*Note*: You can also choose File, New from the Menu bar.)

There are times when you'll want to save an existing workbook under a different file name. For example, you may want to keep different versions of the same workbook on your disk. Or, you may want to use one workbook as a template for future workbooks that are similar in style and format. Rather than retyping an entirely new workbook, you can retrieve an old workbook file, edit the information, and then save it under a different name using the File, Save As command. If you want to replace the old file instead, you use File, Save or click the Save button (▦).

Quick Reference	• CHOOSE: File, Save, or
Saving a File	• CHOOSE: File, Save As, or
	• CLICK: Save button (▦)

Quick Reference	• CHOOSE: File, Close, or
Closing a File	• DOUBLE-CLICK: Control menu for the document window

Quick Reference	• CHOOSE: File, New, or
Opening a New File	• CLICK: New Workbook button (▢)

LEAVING EXCEL

When you are finished using Excel, save your work and exit the program before turning off the computer. If you have made modifications to the workbook and have not saved the changes, Excel asks whether the workbook should be saved or abandoned before exiting the program.

Perform the following steps to finish working with Excel.

1. To exit Excel:
   CHOOSE: File, Exit
   Assuming that no changes were made to the new workbook, the application is closed and you are returned to the Program Manager.

2. To exit Windows:
   CHOOSE: File, Exit
   Rather than using the menu commands, you can double-click the Control menus for both Excel and the Program Manager.

Quick Reference	• CHOOSE: File, Exit, or
Exiting Excel	• DOUBLE-CLICK: Excel's Control menu

SUMMARY

This session introduced you to working with spreadsheet programs, specifically Microsoft Excel for Windows. We began the session exploring the advantages of electronic spreadsheets over manual worksheets, comparing the size of work areas and the speeds at which calculations and corrections are performed. The importance of planning the construction of a spreadsheet was also emphasized.

After you loaded Microsoft Windows and Excel, this session presented an overview of Excel's major components, including the application and document windows. As well, you were introduced to data entry techniques for entering text, numbers, and formulas into the worksheet cells. Because even experts require some assistance now and then, this session also demonstrated the Excel Help facility.

For easy reference, many of the commands and procedures appearing in this session are provided in Table 1.4, the Command Summary.

	Command	*Description*
Table 1.4		
Command Summary	File, New (□)	Creates a new workbook file.
	File, Save (💾)	Saves a workbook file to the disk.
	File, Save As	Saves a workbook file, specifying the file name.
	File, Exit	Leaves Excel.
	Edit, Undo (↶)	Reverses the last commands executed.
	Edit, Clear	Erases the contents and formatting of a cell.
	Help, Contents	Displays a table of contents for the Help facility.

KEY TERMS

application window   In Microsoft Windows, each running application program appears in its own application window. These windows can be sized and moved anywhere on the Windows desktop.

cell   In a spreadsheet program, this marks the intersection of a column and a row.

cell address   The location of a cell on a spreadsheet given by the intersection of a column and a row. Columns are usually labeled using letters. Rows are numbered. A cell address combines the column letter with the row number (for example, B9 or DF134).

cell pointer   The cursor on a spreadsheet that points to a cell. The cell pointer is moved using the arrow keys or the mouse.

document window   In Microsoft Excel, each open workbook file appears in its own document window. These windows can be sized and moved anywhere within the Excel application window.

formulas   Mathematical expressions that define the relationships among various cells in an electronic spreadsheet.

graphical user interface   Software feature that allows the user to select menu options and icons; makes software easier to use and typically employs a mouse.

icons   Pictures that represent the different application programs and processing procedures you can execute. Macintosh programs and Microsoft Windows use icons extensively.

jump terms   In the Windows Help facility, a hypertext phrase that appears green with a solid underline that lets you jump from topic to topic by clicking with the mouse.

Microsoft Windows   Graphical user interface software for IBM and IBM-compatible microcomputers.

mouse   Hand-held input device connected to a microcomputer by a cable; when the mouse is rolled across the desktop, the cursor moves across the screen. Buttons on the mouse allow users to make menu selections and to issue commands.

multitasking   Activity in which more than one task or program is executed at a time. A small amount of each program is processed, and then the CPU moves to the remaining programs, one at a time, processing small parts of each.

Program Manager   The primary window or shell for Microsoft Windows. Applications are launched from the Program Manager.

Undo command   In a software application program, a command that makes it possible to reverse the last command executed.

what-if analysis   Also called *scenario analysis*. The ability to change the values of independent variables and immediately see the effects of those changes on dependent formulas or calculations.

workbook   The Excel file where you create your work. A workbook appears in a document window and may contain worksheets, chart sheets, and programming modules (also called macro sheets.)

WYSIWYG   Acronym for *What You See Is What You Get*. Page description software that allows the user to see the final version of a document on the screen before it is printed out.

EXERCISES

SHORT ANSWER

1. What is the procedure for loading Excel?
2. What is a cell? a cell address?
3. What advantages do electronic spreadsheets have over manual worksheets?
4. Explain the term *context-sensitive help*.
5. How do you reverse the last command executed?
6. Describe the different methods for moving around the worksheet.
7. What is a toolbar? How is it accessed?

8. What is the significance of an ellipsis (...) after a menu option?
9. What is a formula? Provide an example.
10. What must you type first to inform Excel that you are entering a formula?

HANDS-ON

1. This exercise produces a worksheet to help manage your personal credit card balances and limits. The tasks include entering text and numbers, and editing data.

   a. Load Windows and Excel to begin working with a new workbook.
   b. Move the cell pointer to the following cells: (a) A21, (b) K50, (c) IV50, (d) IV16384, (e) AA1000, (f) A1
   c. With your cell pointer in cell A1:
      TYPE: PERSONAL FINANCIAL PLANNER
      PRESS: [Enter]
   d. Enter the following text labels:

Move to Cell	TYPE:
C3	Budget
D3	Actual
A6	VISA
A7	Chevron
A8	AMEX
A9	M/C

   e. Enter the following numbers:

Move to Cell	TYPE:
C6	1200
C7	500
C8	200
C9	75
D6	1200
D7	450
D8	215
D9	135

   f. Change the label in cell A6 from "VISA" to "Discover" by typing over the existing entry.

g. Change the label in cell A8 from "AMEX" to "AMEX Gold" using the mouse to edit the text in the cell.

h. Change the label in cell A9 from "M/C" to "Mastercard."

i. Change the budgeted value for Chevron in cell C7 to 400.

j. Reverse the change in the last step using the Undo button (🔄).

k. Change the Actual value for AMEX Gold in cell D8 to 210.

l. Reverse the change in the last step by pressing (Ctrl)+z.

2. This exercise uses the same worksheet to practice entering formulas.

a. Move to cell A11.

b. TYPE: Total Balances

c. Move to cell C11. Enter a formula that adds the Budget values in column C by typing the formula.

d. Move to cell D11. Enter a formula that adds the Actual values in column D by pointing to the cell references using the mouse.

e. Move to cell E3.

f. TYPE: Variance

g. In cell E6, enter a formula to subtract the actual Discover card balance from the budgeted value.

h. In cell E7, enter a formula to subtract the actual Chevron balance from the budgeted value.

i. Enter formulas to calculate the variance for the remaining cards.

j. Enter a formula to calculate the variance for the Total Balances.

k. Save the workbook as MYPLAN onto the Advantage Diskette. Your worksheet should now appear similar to Figure 1.11.

l. Exit Excel and Windows.

Figure 1.11

The MYPLAN Personal Financial Planner workbook

	A	B	C	D	E	F	G	H
				MYPLAN.XLS				
1	PERSONAL FINANCIAL PLANNER							
2								
3			Budget	Actual	Variance			
4								
5								
6	Discover		1200	1200	0			
7	Chevron		500	450	50			
8	AMEX Gold		200	215	-15			
9	Mastercard		75	135	-60			
10								
11	Total Balances		1975	2000	-25			
12								
13								
14								
15								

Sheet1 / Sheet2 / Sheet3 / Sheet4 / Sheet5

SESSION 2

MICROSOFT EXCEL 5.0: WORKING WITH SPREADSHEETS

Spreadsheets may look complicated, but even a new user can begin to construct one in a short period of time. This session shows you how to set up a spreadsheet and enter text, numbers, and formulas. Once your spreadsheet is created, you can easily modify it and use it over and over.

PREVIEW

When you have completed this session, you will be able to:

Work with cell ranges.
•
Use the SUM function and the AutoSum button.
•
Change the width of a column and the height of a row.
•
Use fonts to enhance cell information.
•
Format numbers and dates in a worksheet.
•
Align information in a cell.
•
Apply borders and shading patterns to cells.
•
Print and preview a workbook.

43

SESSION OUTLINE

WHY THIS SESSION IS IMPORTANT

In this session, we explore the formatting and printing capabilities of Excel. Whether you are creating a personal financial plan or a corporate marketing strategy, a spreadsheet often forms the basis for reports and decision-making. Because the presentation of facts and figures in a workbook is sometimes as important as the information itself, Excel provides several spreadsheet publishing features to help you better communicate your data.

This session also concentrates on improving your efficiency in working with Excel. A sample workbook is created, formatted, customized, enhanced, saved, and, finally, printed. The procedures and commands described in this session are easily applicable to any workbook that you create using Excel.

Before proceeding, make sure the following are true:

1. You have loaded Microsoft Windows and Excel.
2. You have an empty workbook displayed onscreen.
3. Your Advantage Diskette is inserted into the drive. You save your work onto the diskette and retrieve files that have been created for you.

CREATING A NEW WORKBOOK

When Excel is first loaded, an empty workbook called *Book1* appears in the document window. To create a workbook, you enter information into the worksheets labeled from *Sheet1* to *Sheet16* and then save the workbook under a new file name, such as BUDGET94. (*Note*: In Session 4, you learn how to add and delete the sheets in a workbook.) If you've already entered information into *Book1* and would like to create a new workbook, you choose the File, New command or click the New button (☐) on the Standard Toolbar. Because each workbook that you open consumes memory, you should save your work and close all unnecessary documents before creating a new workbook.

In the next two sections, you create the worksheet appearing in Figure 2.1. You will use this worksheet throughout the session to practice several spreadsheet procedures.

Figure 2.1

The Sales
Projections
worksheet

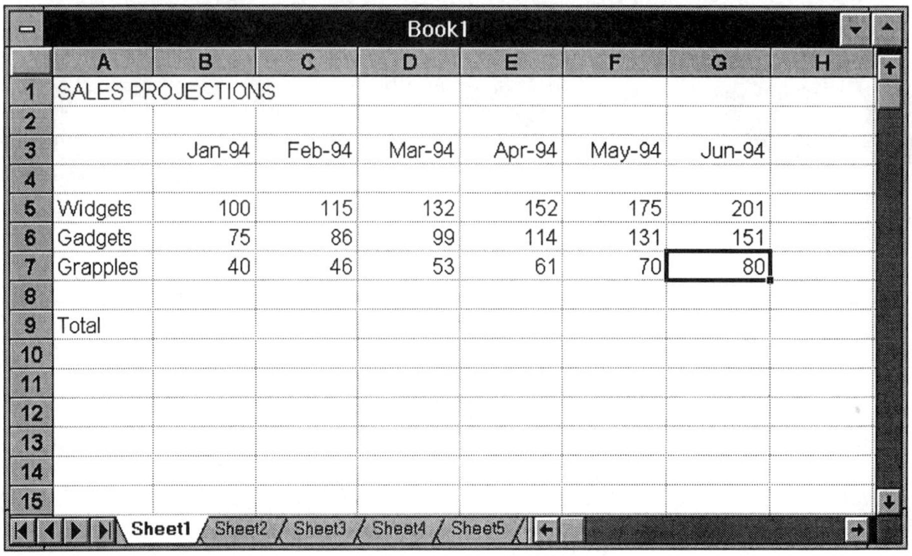

	A	B	C	D	E	F	G	H
1	SALES PROJECTIONS							
2								
3		Jan-94	Feb-94	Mar-94	Apr-94	May-94	Jun-94	
4								
5	Widgets	100	115	132	152	175	201	
6	Gadgets	75	86	99	114	131	151	
7	Grapples	40	46	53	61	70	80	
8								
9	Total							
10								
11								
12								
13								
14								
15								

Sheet1 / Sheet2 / Sheet3 / Sheet4 / Sheet5

Perform the following steps.

1. Enter the following text labels for headings on the worksheet:

Move to Cell	TYPE:
A1	SALES PROJECTIONS
A5	Widgets
A6	Gadgets
A7	Grapples
A9	Total

2. Enter the following dates as column headings:

Move to Cell	TYPE:
B3	Jan-94
C3	Feb-94
D3	Mar-94
E3	Apr-94
F3	May-94
G3	Jun-94

Before completing the data entry for the spreadsheet in Figure 2.1, continue to the next section to learn about cell ranges.

INTRODUCING CELL RANGES

Most Windows programs use the Select and then Do approach for issuing commands. To enhance an Excel worksheet, for example, you select a cell or group of cells—called a **cell range**—and then choose a formatting command. After executing the command, Excel leaves the selected range highlighted for you to perform additional commands. You select a cell range using either the keyboard or the mouse.

A cell range can be a single cell or a rectangular block of worksheet cells. Each cell range has a beginning and an ending cell address. The top left-hand cell is the beginning cell in a range and the bottom right-hand cell is the ending cell in a range. To specify a cell range in a worksheet formula, you enter the two cell addresses separated by a colon (for example, B4:C6). Figure 2.2 illustrates some cell ranges.

Figure 2.2

Cell ranges

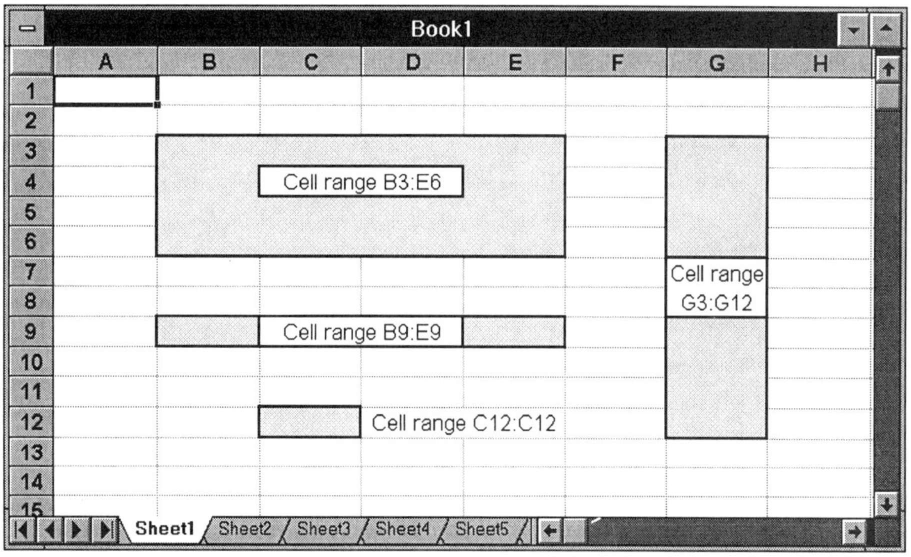

Perform the following steps to practice selecting cell ranges.

1. Move to cell B3.

2. To select the range of cells from B3 to G3 using the keyboard:
    PRESS: (Shift) and hold it down
    PRESS: (→) five times
    If the highlight does not extend from cell B3 to G3, make sure that you
    are holding down the (Shift) key as you press (→).

3. When the range is highlighted, release the (Shift) key.

4. To remove the range selection or highlighting:
    PRESS: an arrow key in any direction, or
    CLICK: any cell

5. To select the range of cells from B5 to G7 using a mouse:
    CLICK: cell B5 and hold down the left mouse button
    DRAG: the mouse pointer down and to the right until you reach G7

6. When the range is highlighted, release the left mouse button. A
    selected range is highlighted in reverse from the rest of the worksheet.
    The exception to this rule is the active cell with the cell pointer, in this
    case cell B5 in the range B5:G7.

7. Cell ranges also make data entry easier and more accurate. As you type
    information into a highlighted cell range, the cell pointer is
    automatically moved to the next available cell when you press (Enter).
    For example, do the following while the cell range remains selected:
    TYPE: 100
    PRESS: (Enter)
    Notice that the cell pointer moves down to cell B6.

8. With the cell range still highlighted, complete the data entry as
    follows:

	B	C	D	E	F	G
5	100	115	132	152	175	201
6	75	86	99	114	131	151
7	40	46	53	61	70	80

9. With the cell range still highlighted, practice moving from cell to cell:
    PRESS: Enter to move down one cell at a time; when you reach the bottom cell, the cell pointer moves to the top of the next column
    PRESS: Shift+Enter to move up one cell at a time; when you reach the top cell, the cell pointer moves to the previous column
    PRESS: Tab to move right one cell; when you reach the rightmost cell in a row, the cell pointer moves to the next row
    PRESS: Shift+Tab to move left one cell; when you reach the leftmost cell, the cell pointer moves to the previous row

10. To remove the highlighting and return to cell A1:
    PRESS: Ctrl+Home

Quick Reference *Selecting a Range of Cells Using the Mouse*	1. Click once on the cell in the top left-hand corner of the range. 2. With the left mouse button depressed, drag the mouse pointer and extend the highlight to the bottom right-hand corner of the range. 3. Release the mouse button.

Quick Reference *Selecting a Range of Cells Using the Keyboard*	1. Position the cell pointer in the top left-hand corner of the cell range. 2. PRESS: Shift key and hold it down 3. Extend the highlight over the desired group of cells using the arrow keys (←, →, ↑, and ↓). 4. Release the Shift key.

SPELL-CHECKING A WORKSHEET

This section introduces the Spell Checker for correcting typographical errors and misspellings. You can perform a spelling check on a particular cell range, a single sheet, several sheets, or the entire workbook. When a spelling check is requested, Excel begins scanning the cells with textual information. Each word is compared to entries in Excel's main dictionary. If the word is not found, Excel attempts to find a match in a custom dictionary that you create.

Perform the following steps.

1. Move to cell A2.

2. Enter a misspelled word:
    TYPE: Summury
    PRESS: (Enter)

3. PRESS: (Ctrl)+(Home) to move to the top of the worksheet

4. To begin the spelling check:
    CHOOSE: Tools, Spelling
    (*Note*: You can also click the Spelling button (⬛) on the Standard
    toolbar to start a spelling check.) When Excel comes across the first
    misspelled word, it displays the dialog box in Figure 2.3 and waits for
    further instructions:

Figure 2.3

Spelling dialog
box

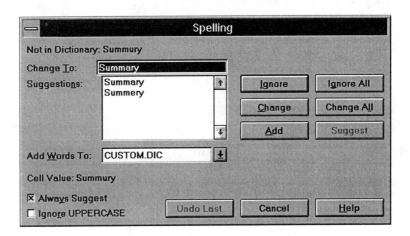

5. You have several options when the Spell Checker cannot find a word:
    • Highlight the correctly spelled word in the Suggestions list box and
      then select the Change command button.
    • Type the correct spelling of the word in the Change To text box
      and then select the Change command button.
    • If the word is spelled correctly and not frequently used, select the
      Ignore or Ignore All buttons to proceed to the next word.
    • If the word is spelled correctly and frequently used, select the Add
      button to add it to the custom dictionary.

    To correct the spelling of Summary and proceed:
    SELECT: Change command button

6. Continue the spelling check for the remainder of the worksheet. When
    it has completed, a message box will appear asking for confirmation:
    PRESS: (Enter) or CLICK: OK

7.   PRESS: Ctrl + Home to move to the top of the worksheet

8.   Save the workbook as SALES94 onto the Advantage Diskette.

Quick Reference *Spell-Checking a Worksheet*	1. CHOOSE: Tools, Spelling 2. When a misspelled word is located, Excel suggests alternative spellings. Highlight a suggestion and select the Change button or select Ignore to continue without modification. 3. When a technical term or proper name cannot be found, add the word to the custom dictionary by selecting the Add button.

CALCULATING TOTALS

A few numbers on a worksheet can be summed quite easily with a simple addition formula. However, imagine the time it would take to sum a column of 100 numbers with a formula such as =A1+A2+A3...+A99. Fortunately, Excel has anticipated many of these repetitive operations and provides a library of electronic shortcuts called **functions**, organized into the following categories:

- Database
- Date & Time
- Financial
- Information
- Logical

- Lookup & Reference
- Math & Trig
- Statistical
- Text

The statistical functions are the most commonly used, enabling you to sum or average a range of numbers, count cell entries, and extract maximum and minimum results from a range of data. This section introduces the **SUM function** which is used as a replacement for long addition formulas. To enter the SUM function into a cell, you can type the expression or click the AutoSum button (Σ) on the Standard toolbar.

THE SUM FUNCTION

The first step in using the SUM function is to move to the cell where you want the result to appear. Functions, like formulas, begin with an equal sign to inform Excel to expect a function name as opposed to a text label.

The syntax for the SUM command is =SUM(cell range), where the cell range is the block of cells to be summed. You can enter the cell range by typing the cell addresses or by highlighting the block of cells.

The objective of the following exercise is to demonstrate these two methods for entering the SUM function. Normally, you would not use a different method to sum each column. However, this example provides an opportunity to practice some important skills. Perform the following steps.

1. Move to cell B9.

2. To calculate the total sales for the month of January, enter the SUM function by typing the cell addresses:
   TYPE: =sum(b5:b7)
   PRESS: [→]
   The value 215 appears in the cell. (*Note*: You can enter the function name and cell range using uppercase or lowercase letters.)

3. To calculate the total sales for February, enter the SUM function into cell C9 by pointing to the cell range using the keyboard:
   TYPE: =sum(
   PRESS: [↑] four times to move to cell C5
   PRESS: [Shift] and hold down
   PRESS: [↓] twice to extend the range to cell C7
   TYPE:) and release the [Shift] key
   PRESS: [→]
   The number 247 appears in cell C9.

4. To calculate the total sales for March, enter the SUM function into cell D9 by pointing to the cell range using the mouse:
   TYPE: =sum(
   CLICK: cell D5 and hold down the left mouse button
   DRAG: mouse pointer to cell D7 and then release the mouse button
   TYPE:)
   PRESS: [→]
   The number 284 appears in cell D9.

5. SELECT: cell range from E9 to G9

6. To calculate the total sales for April through June, enter the SUM function once and copy the formula to the remaining cells in the range using a keyboard shortcut:
    TYPE: =sum(e5:e7)
    PRESS: [Ctrl]+[Enter]
    When you press [Ctrl]+[Enter], Excel copies the entry in the active cell to the remaining cells in the highlighted range; in this case, F9 and G9.

THE AUTOSUM BUTTON

Rather than entering an addition formula or the SUM function manually, you can use the AutoSum button (Σ) to automatically sum a cell range. To AutoSum a cell range, you position the cell pointer where you want the result to appear and click the AutoSum button (Σ) once. Excel enters the SUM function with its best guess of the desired cell range. If the range is correct, press [Enter] to complete the entry. You can also double-click the AutoSum button (Σ) to enter the SUM function into the active cell.

Let's complete the Sales Projections worksheet by calculating the total sales for each product.

1. Move to cell H3.

2. TYPE: Total

3. Move to cell H9.

4. To calculate the total sales for all products:
    CLICK: AutoSum button (Σ)
    Verify that the cell range appearing in the cell and in the Formula bar is correct before proceeding to the next step.

5. To proceed, you can press [Enter] or do the following:
    CLICK: AutoSum button (Σ) a second time

6. To calculate the total sales for each individual product, select the cell range from H5 to H7. Ensure that the entire range is highlighted.

7. CLICK: AutoSum button (Σ)
    The SUM function is automatically entered for all three highlighted cells. Your worksheet should now appear similar to Figure 2.4.

Figure 2.4

SALES94 after
entering the SUM
function and using
the AutoSum button
(Σ)

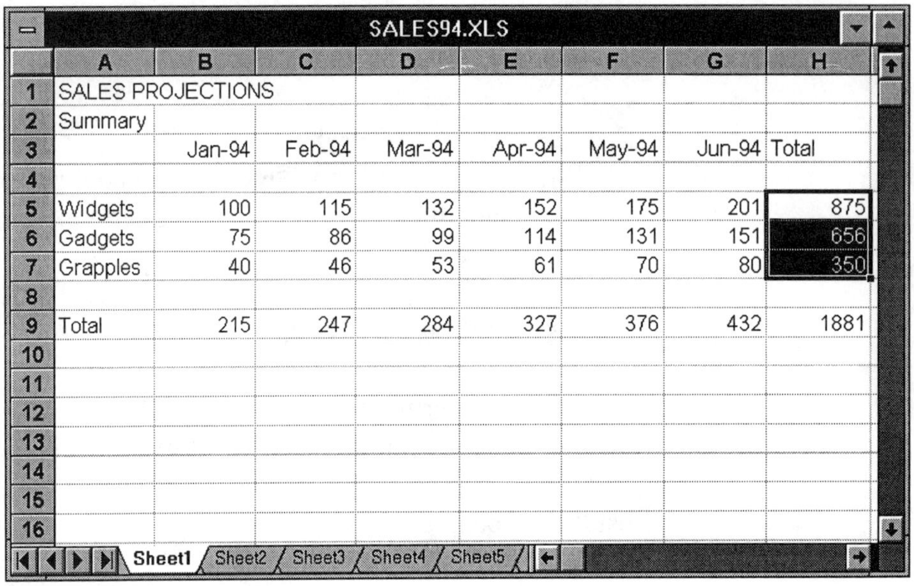

	A	B	C	D	E	F	G	H
1	SALES PROJECTIONS							
2	Summary							
3		Jan-94	Feb-94	Mar-94	Apr-94	May-94	Jun-94	Total
4								
5	Widgets	100	115	132	152	175	201	875
6	Gadgets	75	86	99	114	131	151	656
7	Grapples	40	46	53	61	70	80	350
8								
9	Total	215	247	284	327	376	432	1881

SALES94.XLS — Sheet1 / Sheet2 / Sheet3 / Sheet4 / Sheet5

8. Using the mouse, click each of the cells H5, H6, and H7 and read the cell references in the Formula bar. Ensure that each SUM function sums the correct cell range.

9. Save the SALES94 workbook to the Advantage Diskette.

Quick Reference
AutoSum Button
1. Move the cell pointer to where you want the result to appear.
2. CLICK: AutoSum button (Σ)

CHANGING COLUMN WIDTHS

You can increase the **column width** of your worksheet columns to allow for long text labels, numbers, and date formats. To change a column's width from the default or standard width, move the cell pointer to any cell in the desired column and then choose the Format, Column, Width command from the Menu bar. The dialog box in Figure 2.5 appears:

Figure 2.5

Column Width
dialog box

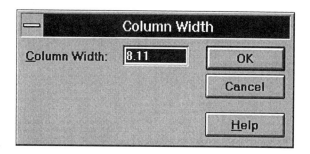

In the Column Width text box, you type the desired width and press (Enter)
or click on OK. To change the width of more than one column at a time,
you highlight cells within the columns (on any row) before you issue the
command. You can also choose the Format, Column, AutoFit Selection
command to have Excel calculate the best width for the column based on
its entries. As with most procedures, there are keyboard and mouse
methods for changing a column's width. Using a mouse, you modify a
column's width by dragging the column borders within the frame area.

Perform the following steps.

1. Move to cell A1.

2. To change the width of column A to 10 characters:
   CHOOSE: Format, Column, Width

3. In the Column Width text box, enter the number of characters:
   TYPE: 10
   PRESS: (Enter) or CLICK: OK
   The column's width is changed and you are returned to the worksheet.

4. To change the width of column B to 12 characters using the mouse,
   first move the mouse pointer into the column frame area where the
   column letters (A, B, and so on) appear.

5. Position the mouse pointer over the borderline between column B and
   column C. The mouse pointer changes shape from a cross to a black
   vertical line split by a black horizontal double-headed arrow.

6. CLICK: the borderline and hold down the mouse button
   DRAG: the mouse pointer to the right to increase the width to 12
   (*Hint*: The width is displayed in the Name box of the Formula bar.)

7. Release the mouse button.

8. To concurrently change multiple columns to the same width, you must first select the columns by dragging the mouse pointer over the column letters in the frame area. For this step, select columns B through H using the mouse.

9. Let's let Excel choose the best column width:
    CHOOSE: Format, Column, AutoFit Selection
    Although the columns are adjusted to best fit their cell entries, they appear quite narrow. In the next step, you increase their widths.

10. With the columns still selected, drag any border in the highlighted frame area to increase the width of all columns to 8 characters.

Quick Reference	1. Select a cell in the column that you want to format.
Changing a	2. CHOOSE: Format, Column, Width
Column's Width	3. Type the desired column width in the text box.
	4. PRESS: Enter or CLICK: OK

CHANGING ROW HEIGHTS

You can change the **row height** of any worksheet row to customize borders and line spacing. To change a row's height, move the cell pointer to any cell in the desired row and then choose Format, Row, Height from the Menu bar. The dialog box in Figure 2.6 appears:

Figure 2.6

Row Height dialog box

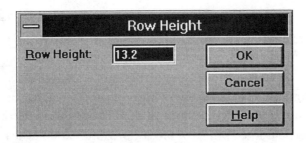

In the Row Height text box, you type the desired height in points and press Enter or click OK. (*Note:* There are 72 points in one inch and a standard row height measures approximately 13 points.) To change the height of more than one row at a time, you highlight the rows in the frame area before you issue the command. Similarly to changing a column's width, you can use a mouse to drag the row borders within the frame area to increase or decrease a row's height.

Perform the following steps.

1. Move to cell A1.

2. To change the height of Row 1 to 25 points (approximately 3/8 inch), issue the formatting command:
   CHOOSE: Format, Row, Height

3. In the Row Height text box, enter a number for the height in points:
   TYPE: 25
   PRESS: (Enter) or CLICK: OK
   The row's height is changed, and you are returned to the worksheet.

4. To change the height of Row 3 to 21 points using a mouse, first move the mouse pointer into the frame area where the row numbers appear.

5. Position the mouse pointer over the borderline between Row 3 and Row 4. The mouse pointer changes shapes from a cross to a black horizontal line split by a black vertical double-headed arrow.

6. CLICK: the borderline and hold down the mouse button
   DRAG: the mouse pointer down to increase the row height to 21
   (*Hint*: The height is displayed in the Name box of the Formula bar.)

7. Release the mouse button.

8. To change multiple rows to the same height, you must first select the rows by dragging the mouse in the frame area. For this step, select the range from row 5 to row 9.

9. To change the row height to 16 points:
   CHOOSE: Format, Row, Height
   TYPE: 16
   PRESS: (Enter) or CLICK: OK

10. Save the SALES94 workbook to the Advantage Diskette.

Unlike column widths, row heights are automatically adjusted to their best fit according to the font size of entries in the row. However, you can still modify the spacing in your worksheets by adjusting row heights manually.

Quick Reference	1. Select a cell in the row to format.
Changing a Row's	2. CHOOSE: Format, Row, Height
Height	3. Type the desired row height in the text box.
	4. PRESS: ⌗Enter⌗ or CLICK: OK

FORMATTING YOUR WORKSHEET

With Excel's spreadsheet publishing capabilities, you can enhance your worksheets with a variety of fonts, borders, and shading. You can also format numbers to display currency and percentage symbols and to specify the number of decimal places. The combination of these features enables you to produce professional-looking reports and presentations using Excel.

SELECTING CELL RANGES

To format your worksheet, you first select the desired cells to enhance and then issue a formatting command. To this point in the guide, you've learned how to select a single cell and a single block of cells called a range. There are several additional methods for selecting cells in a worksheet that will improve your productivity. For example, you can select multiple cell ranges in different areas of a worksheet and then apply a single command to format them all. Some common selection methods are provided below.

- To apply formatting changes to an entire worksheet, select the worksheet by pressing ⌗Ctrl⌗+a or by clicking once on the Select All button (▭), located in the top left-hand corner of the frame area.

- To select multiple cell ranges, select the first cell range as usual and then hold down the ⌗Ctrl⌗ key as you select the additional cell ranges using the mouse.

- To select a cell range that spans several pages of the worksheet, select the first cell (top left-hand corner of the range) and then scroll to the last cell (bottom right-hand corner of the range) using the scroll bars. When the last cell is visible, press and hold down the (**Shift**) key and click the cell. All the cells in between the first and last are highlighted.

Because a cell range remains highlighted after issuing a command, you can choose additional formatting commands without having to re-select cells. To remove the highlighting, you press an arrow key or click on any cell in the worksheet.

USING FONTS

One of the most effective means of enhancing a worksheet is to vary the **fonts**—that is, the **typefaces** and point sizes—that are used in titles, column headings, row labels, and other worksheet cells. Although fonts are effective at drawing the reader's attention to specific topics, don't feel that you must use every font in each worksheet. Remember, a worksheet must be easy to read and understand, and too many fonts are distracting.

To enhance your worksheet, you select the cell or range of cells to format and then issue the Format, Cells command from the menu. (*Hint*: You can also select the Format Cells command from a shortcut menu.) For fonts and styles, you select the Font tab by clicking on it using the mouse. After making the desired selections from the dialog box, you press (**Enter**) or click the OK command button. Rather than accessing the menu, you can click buttons on the Formatting toolbar: Font ([Arial ▼]), Font Size ([10 ▼]), Bold (**B**), Italic (*I*), and Underline (**U**). These buttons provide single-step access to the most popular features found in the Format Cells dialog box (Figure 2.7).

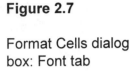

Figure 2.7

Format Cells dialog
box: Font tab

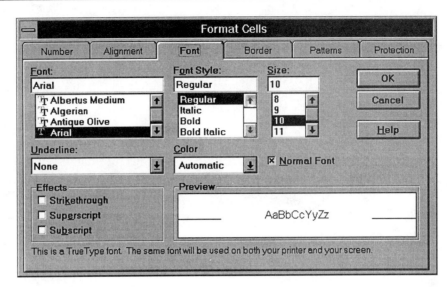

Perform the following steps to change fonts and styles in the worksheet.

1. SELECT: cell range from B3 to H3

2. To emphasize the column headings, make the dates bold:
    CLICK: Bold button (**B**)

3. SELECT: cell range from A5 to A9

4. To italicize the product names:
    CLICK: Italics button (*I*)

5. SELECT: cell A1

6. To enhance the title:
    CHOOSE: Format, Cells
    SELECT: Font tab

7. SELECT: Times New Roman from the Font list box
    SELECT: Bold Italic from the Font Style list box
    SELECT: 18 from the Size list box
    PRESS: (Enter) or CLICK: OK

8. SELECT: cell A2

9. To enhance the subtitle using the Formatting toolbar:
   SELECT: Times New Roman from the Font drop-down list box
   ([Arial ▼])
   SELECT: 14 from the Font Size drop-down list box ([10 ▼])
   (*Hint*: To display the options in a drop-down list, you click the down
   arrow adjacent to the drop-down list on the toolbar.) Your screen
   should now appear similar to Figure 2.8.

Figure 2.8

Applying fonts to
the worksheet

	A	B	C	D	E	F	G	H
1	*SALES PROJECTIONS*							
2	Summary							
3		Jan-94	Feb-94	Mar-94	Apr-94	May-94	Jun-94	Total
4								
5	*Widgets*	100	115	132	152	175	201	875
6	*Gadgets*	75	86	99	114	131	151	656
7	*Grapples*	40	46	53	61	70	80	350
8								
9	*Total*	215	247	284	327	376	432	1881

SALES94.XLS — Sheet1 / Sheet2 / Sheet3 / Sheet4 / Sheet5

Quick Reference *Using Fonts*	1. SELECT: the cell or cell range that you want to format
	2. CHOOSE: Format, Cells command
	3. SELECT: Font tab
	4. SELECT: a Font, Font Style, Size, Color, and Effects
	5. PRESS: [Enter] or CLICK: OK.

FORMATTING VALUES

Numeric formats improve the appearance and readability of numbers in a
worksheet by inserting dollar signs, commas, percentage symbols, and
decimal places. Although the number appears differently on the worksheet
when formatting is applied, the value in the Formula bar does not
change—only the appearance of the number changes. In addition to dollar
figures and percentages, Excel stores date and time entries as values and
allows you to customize their display in the worksheet.

To enhance your worksheet with value formatting, select the desired cell range and then issue the Format, Cells command. (*Hint*: You can also select the Format Cells command from a shortcut menu.) When the dialog box appears, select the Number tab to display a variety of numeric formatting options. Figure 2.9 provides an example of the Format Cells dialog box with the Number tab selected.

Figure 2.9

Format Cells dialog box: Number tab

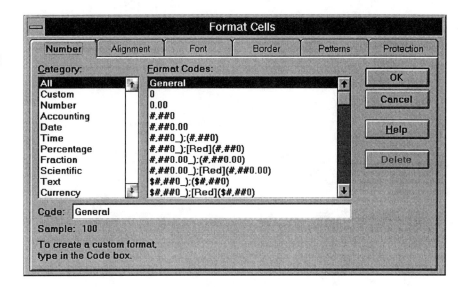

You choose a format by selecting an option in the Category list box and then highlighting an option in the Format Codes list box. When completed, you press (Enter) or click on OK. You can also format values by clicking the following buttons on the Formatting toolbar: Currency Style ($), Percent Style (%), Comma Style (,), Increase Decimal, and Decrease Decimal. These buttons provide single-step access to the most popular features found in the Format Cells dialog box

Perform the following steps.

1. SELECT: cell range from B9 to H9

2. To display the dialog box of numeric formatting options:
    RIGHT-CLICK: the highlighted cell range
    CHOOSE: Format Cells
    SELECT: Number tab

3. To view the currency formatting options:
    SELECT: Currency in the Category list box

4. To select a currency format with a dollar sign, commas, and two decimal places:
SELECT: $#,##0.00_);($#,##0.00) from the Format Codes list box
PRESS: [Enter] or CLICK: OK
(*Note*: The symbols on the left of the semicolon represent the positive format for a number and the symbols on the right represent the negative format. For example, the number 1000 would appear as $1,000.00 and the number –1000 would appear as ($1,000.00), using this format.)

5. Increase the width of column H to 10 characters:
SELECT: cell H9
CHOOSE: Format, Column, Width
TYPE: 10
PRESS: [Enter] or CLICK: OK

6. SELECT: cell range from B5 to H7.

7. To select a number format with commas and two decimal places:
CLICK: Comma Style button ([,])
CLICK: Increase Decimal button ([.00]) twice

Upon selecting a numeric or date formatting option, a cell may display a series of pound signs (########). This is Excel's way of informing you that the cell is not wide enough to display the value using the selected format. Your options are to either increase the column's width or select a different numeric format.

Quick Reference	1. SELECT: the cell or cell range that you want to format
Formatting	2. CHOOSE: Format, Cells
Numbers and Dates	3. SELECT: Number tab
	4. SELECT: a format from the Category and Format Codes list boxes
	5. PRESS: [Enter] or CLICK: OK.

ALIGNING A CELL'S CONTENTS

Excel automatically aligns text against the left edge of a cell and values against the right edge. However, you can easily change the **cell alignment** for any type of information in the worksheet. Using the menu, you choose the Format, Cells command and make selections from the Alignment tab in the dialog box (Figure 2.10). Using the Formatting toolbar, you click the Align Left (▤), Center (▥), Align Right (▤), and Center Across Columns (▦) buttons to align cell information.

Figure 2.10

Format Cells dialog box: Alignment tab

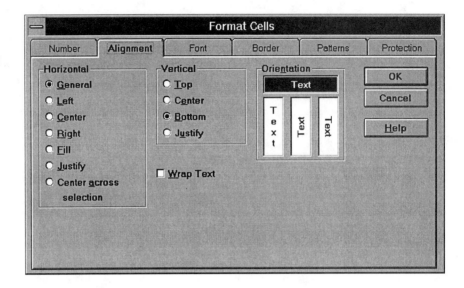

Perform the following steps.

1. SELECT: cell range from B3 to H3

2. To center the date column headings:
   CLICK: Center button (▥)

3. SELECT: cell range from A5 to A9

4. To right align the product or row headings:
   CLICK: Align Right button (▤)

5. To center the title in A1 across the width of the worksheet:
   SELECT: cell range from A1 to H1

6. CLICK: Center Across Selection button (▦)

7. Move to cell A1. Notice that the title appears in the Formula bar. Even though the worksheet displays the title between columns A and H, the title remains in cell A1. Your screen should now appear similar to Figure 2.11.

8. Save the SALES94 worksheet to the Advantage Diskette.

Figure 2.11

Aligning information
in SALES94

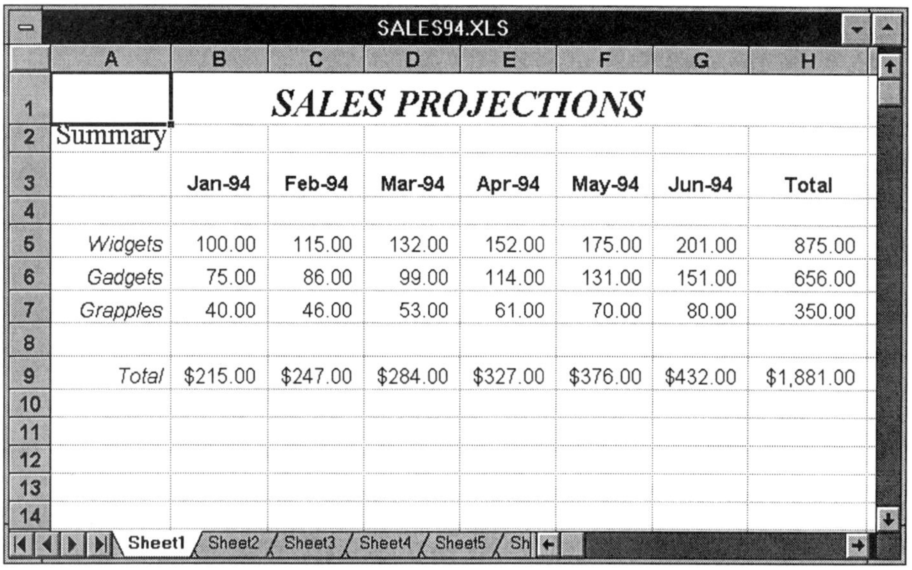

	A	B	C	D	E	F	G	H
1		SALES PROJECTIONS						
2	Summary							
3		Jan-94	Feb-94	Mar-94	Apr-94	May-94	Jun-94	Total
4								
5	Widgets	100.00	115.00	132.00	152.00	175.00	201.00	875.00
6	Gadgets	75.00	86.00	99.00	114.00	131.00	151.00	656.00
7	Grapples	40.00	46.00	53.00	61.00	70.00	80.00	350.00
8								
9	Total	$215.00	$247.00	$284.00	$327.00	$376.00	$432.00	$1,881.00
10								
11								
12								
13								
14								

Sheet1 / Sheet2 / Sheet3 / Sheet4 / Sheet5 / Sh

Quick Reference	1. SELECT: the cell or cell range that you want to format
Changing a Cell's	2. CHOOSE: Format, Cells and SELECT: Alignment tab, or
Alignment	CLICK: Align Left (▤), Center (▤), Align Right (▤), or Center Across Selection (▦) buttons on the Formatting toolbar

ADDING BORDERS AND SHADING CELLS

The gridlines that appear in the document window are non-printing lines, provided only to help you line up information. To emphasize your worksheet, you can add your own borders, underlines, and shading to cells. Borders are used to separate data into logical sections and enhance titles. As well, these features provide publishing capabilities for creating invoice forms, memos, and tables.

To add borders and shaded patterns to your worksheet, select the desired cell or cell range and issue the Format, Cells command. In the dialog box that appears, select the Border tab to display the dialog box in Figure 2.12 or the Patterns tab to display the dialog box page shown in Figure 2.13. When you are finished making selections from the two pages, you press (Enter) or click on the OK command button. You can also click the Borders drop-down list (▦) on the Formatting toolbar to quickly apply borders to a selection.

Figure 2.12

Format Cells dialog
box: Border tab

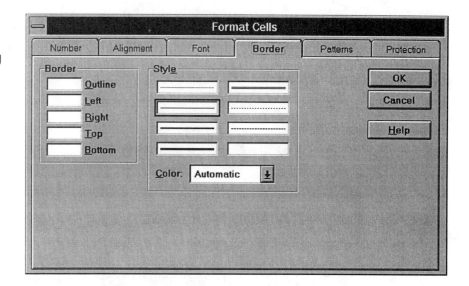

Figure 2.13

Format Cells dialog
box: Patterns tab

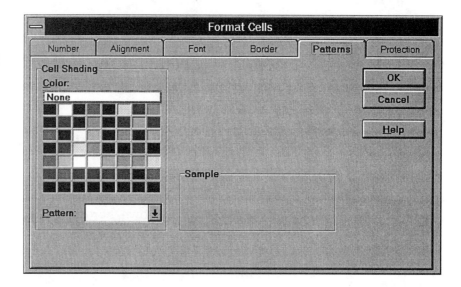

Perform the following steps to practice creating borders and shading cells.

1. SELECT: cell range from B3 to H3

2. To add a border to the worksheet:
    CLICK: down arrow adjacent to the Borders drop-down list ([⊞]▾)
    You should see a list of sample border formats appear. (*CAUTION*:
    Make sure that you click the down arrow and not the button itself.)

3. SELECT: an outline border (in the bottom right-hand corner of the list)
    The formatting is immediately applied to the selection.

4. SELECT: cell range from B9 to H9

5. To add two different borders to this range:
   CHOOSE: Format, Cells
   SELECT: Border tab
   SELECT: Top in the Border group
   SELECT: a single line (second from the top) in the Style group
   SELECT: Bottom in the Border group
   SELECT: a double line (top of the second column) in the Style group
   PRESS: (Enter) or CLICK: OK

6. To shade a group of cells:
   SELECT: cell range from B3 to H3
   RIGHT-CLICK: the selected range
   CHOOSE: Format Cells
   SELECT: Patterns tab
   SELECT: down arrow adjacent to the Patterns drop-down list box
   SELECT: the pattern shown in the top right-hand corner
   PRESS: (Enter) or CLICK: OK

7. In order to get a full appreciation of fonts and borders, Excel allows you to temporarily remove the **gridlines** from the worksheet. This provides a more accurate view of how the worksheet will look when printed. To temporarily remove the gridlines from your worksheet:
   PRESS: (Ctrl)+(Home)
   CHOOSE: Tools, Options
   SELECT: View tab
   SELECT: Gridlines check box until no × appears
   PRESS: (Enter) or CLICK: OK
   (*Note*: Although this option allows you to better view your worksheet, changing the screen display is entirely independent from choosing print options. Print options for gridlines and headings must still be specified, as explained later in this session.)

   Your worksheet should now appear similar to Figure 2.14.

Figure 2.14

The SALES94 worksheet after applying borders and shading and removing the gridlines

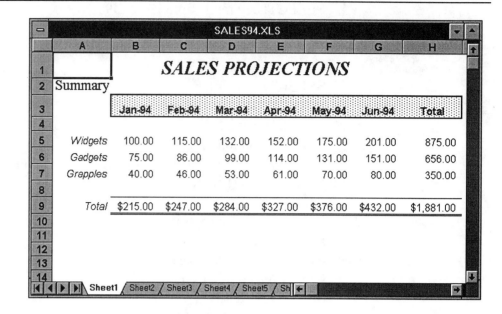

8. To return the display to normal:
    CHOOSE: Tools, Options
    SELECT: View tab (if it is not already selected)
    SELECT: Gridlines check box until an × appears
    PRESS: (Enter) or CLICK: OK

Quick Reference	1. SELECT: the cell or cell range that you want to format
Adding Borders and	2. CHOOSE: Format, Cells
Patterns	3. SELECT: Border tab to specify border lines
	4. SELECT: Patterns tab to specify a shading level or color
	5. PRESS: (Enter) or CLICK: OK

COPYING FORMATTING OPTIONS

Excel's Format Painter button (🖌) lets you copy the formatting styles from one area in your worksheet to another. To copy a cell's formatting, you select the cell and click the Format Painter button (🖌). To apply the formatting, you drag the paintbrush mouse pointer across the cell range that you want formatted. When you release the mouse button, the formatting styles are copied from the original selection to your new selection. Not only does this feature increase your productivity, it ensures consistency among the formatting of cells in your worksheet.

Let's practice—perform the following steps.

1. To practice copying styles, let's format a cell with new options:
    SELECT: cell B5
    CLICK: Decrease Decimal button (![]) twice
    The entry in cell B5 will now appear as 100.

2. To copy this formatting change to the rest of the values:
    CLICK: Format Painter button (![])

3. Move the mouse pointer into the document window. Notice that the mouse pointer is now a cross with a paintbrush.

4. SELECT: the cell range from B5 to H9

5. Release the mouse button. Notice that all the values in the range are formatted with the same features as cell B5, including no decimal places and no borders.

6. To undo the last operation:
    CLICK: Undo button (![])
    PRESS: [Esc] to remove the dashed marquee around cell B5
    PRESS: [Ctrl]+[Home] to return to cell A1

Quick Reference	1. SELECT: the cell whose formatting you want to copy
Copying a Cell's	2. CLICK: Format Painter button (![]) on the Formatting toolbar
Formatting	3. SELECT: the cell range that you want formatted
	4. Release the mouse button to complete the operation.

REMOVING FORMATTING OPTIONS

If you want to remove the formatting features applied to an area on your worksheet, select the cell or range of cells and then choose the Edit, Clear command from the menu. On the cascading menu that appears, you select the Formats command. To demonstrate, perform the following steps.

1. SELECT: cell A1

2. To remove the formatting for this cell:
    CHOOSE: Edit, Clear, Formats
    Notice that the cell's formatting is stripped while its contents are left intact.

3. To undo the last command:
    CLICK: Undo button (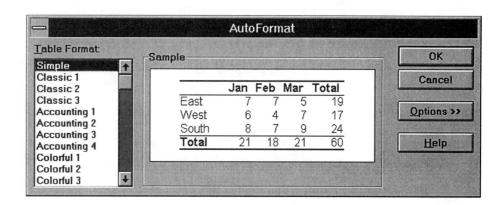)

Quick Reference	1.	SELECT: a cell or cell range
Removing a Cell's	2.	CHOOSE: Edit, Clear, Formats
Formatting		

USING THE AUTOFORMAT COMMAND

The AutoFormat feature lets you apply a predefined table format, complete with numeric formats, alignments, borders, shading, and colors, to a group of cells on your worksheet. This feature assumes that your data is organized in the worksheet as a table, with labels running down the left column and across the top row. To display the AutoFormat dialog box (Figure 2.15), choose the Format, AutoFormat command from the menu.

Figure 2.15

AutoFormat dialog box

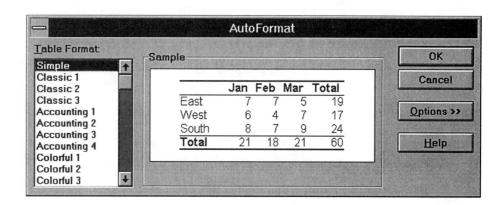

To view a sample of each format, select the options in the Table Format list box. When you find a table format that you like, press **Enter** or click on OK. Now let's apply a few different formats to your worksheet. Perform the following steps.

1. SELECT: cell range from A3 to H9

2. To display the AutoFormat dialog box:
    CHOOSE: Format, AutoFormat

3. Under the Table Format list box:
   SELECT: Colorful 2
   PRESS: (Enter) or CLICK: OK

4. To remove the highlighting from the range:
   SELECT: cell A1

5. Practice choosing some of the other table format options from the AutoFormat dialog box.

6. Close the SALES94 workbook and do not save the changes.
   (*Hint*: CHOOSE: File, Close and answer the prompts that appear.)

Quick Reference *Using AutoFormat*	1. SELECT: the cell or cell range that you want to format 2. CHOOSE: Format, AutoFormat 3. SELECT: *a table format option* 4. PRESS: (Enter) or CLICK: OK

OPENING AN EXISTING WORKBOOK

Excel workbooks are typically stored on floppy diskettes or on the hard disk. To modify or print an existing worksheet, you must first load the file from storage into the computer's memory. You can choose the File, Open command to retrieve an existing workbook from the disk or click the Open button (🖼) on the Standard toolbar. Once the Open dialog box is displayed, you can either type the full name of the file or select the appropriate options from the list boxes.

Perform the following steps to retrieve the SALES94 workbook.

1. Ensure that the Advantage Diskette is placed into the diskette drive.

2. CLICK: Open button (🖼)

3. To display the files on the Advantage Diskette:
    CLICK: Drives drop-down list box
    SELECT: a:
    (*Note*: If you are using a drive other than drive A: for the Advantage Diskette, you must substitute your drive letter in the instructions.) Excel accesses the Advantage Diskette and displays your files in the File Name list box. Your screen should appear similar to Figure 2.16.

Figure 2.16

Open dialog box

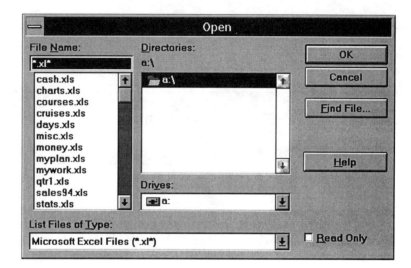

4. To load the SALES94 workbook, scroll the list box until you can see the SALES94 file and then do the following:
    DOUBLE-CLICK: SALES94.XLS in the File Name list box
    The SALES94 workbook reappears in the document area.

Quick Reference	1.	CHOOSE: File, Open or CLICK: Open button (⬚)
Opening an	2.	SELECT: the disk drive, directory, and file name using the list boxes
Existing Worksheet	3.	PRESS: Enter or CLICK: OK

PRINTING THE WORKBOOK

This section introduces the commands for printing a workbook, including options for setting up the page and previewing the output. Excel uses the Windows **Print Manager** for managing printer resources, similar to most Windows applications. When you send a worksheet to the printer, it is intercepted by the Print Manager and placed in a **print queue**. This queue allows you to send multiple pages or multiple worksheets to the printer without having to wait until the printer finishes printing the previous page.

DEFINING THE PAGE LAYOUT

You define the page layout settings for printing a workbook using the File, Page Setup command. In the dialog box that appears, you specify **margins**, **headers**, **footers**, and whether or not gridlines and headings should appear on the final printed document. To make the process more manageable, Excel organizes the page layout settings under four tabs in the Page Setup dialog box:

PAGE TAB   The Page tab lets you specify the paper size and the workbook's print orientation (for example, portrait or landscape.). To print more information on a page, you can also adjust or scale the print size to be smaller than normal using this tab. For example, you can reduce the print size to 50% to fit twice as much information on each page.

MARGINS TAB   You specify the top, bottom, left, and right margins using this tab in the Page Setup dialog box. Unless otherwise noted, you enter all measurements in inches. Excel also provides options for centering the worksheet range on the printed page, both horizontally and vertically.

HEADER/FOOTER TAB   You use a header and footer to print static information at the top and bottom of each page, respectively. Excel provides several predefined headers and footers or you can customize your own using special symbols and formatting styles.

SHEET TAB   You specify what you want printed using the Sheet tab. Besides specifying the actual print area, you tell Excel whether to print the gridlines or row and column headings. Excel also lets you use print titles that repeat at the top of each page. Print titles are dynamic and relate directly to the print area, unlike headers which are static text.

In this section, you define the page layout for the SALES94 worksheet. Perform the following steps.

1. To begin specifying the page layout settings:
   CHOOSE: File, Page Setup
   SELECT: Page tab
   The Page Setup dialog box appears as shown in Figure 2.17.

Figure 2.17

Page Setup dialog
box: Page tab

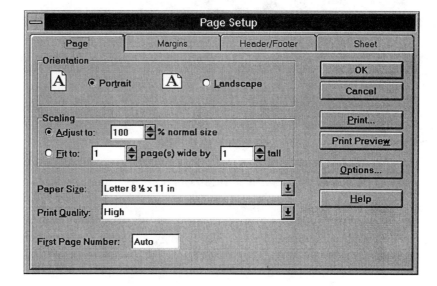

2. Make the following selections:
   SELECT: Portrait in the Orientation group
   SELECT: Adjust to 100% normal size in the Scaling group
   SELECT: Letter 8 ½ × 11 in for the Paper Size

3. To specify the margins:
   SELECT: Margins tab
   The Page Setup dialog box appears as shown in Figure 2.18.

Figure 2.18

Page Setup dialog
box: Margins tab

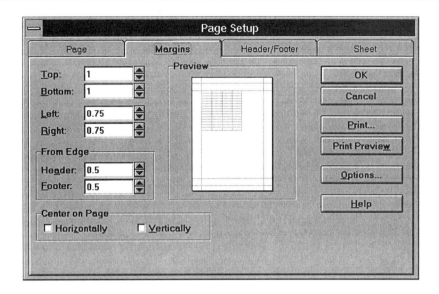

4. Make the following selections:
    SELECT: 1.5 inches for the Top margin
    SELECT: 1.5 inches for the Bottom margin
    SELECT: 1 inch for the Left margin
    SELECT: 1 inch for the Right margin
    (*Hint*: To increase and decrease the margin values, you click the up
    and down triangles that appear to the right of each text box.)

5. To center the worksheet between the left and right margins:
    SELECT: Horizontally check box in the Center on Page group

6. To specify a header and a footer:
    SELECT: Header/Footer tab
    The Page Setup dialog box appears as shown in Figure 2.19.

Figure 2.19

Page Setup dialog
box: Header/Footer
tab

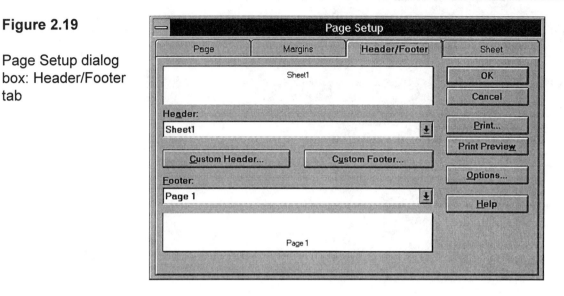

7. To create a custom header:
    SELECT: (none) from the Header drop-down list box
    SELECT: Custom Header command button
    Figure 2.20 shows the Header dialog box and labels the buttons used
    for inserting information into the different sections.

Figure 2.20

Custom Header
dialog box

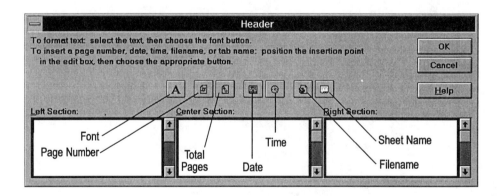

8. To create a header that prints the current date against the right margin:
    SELECT: Right Section by clicking in it once with the mouse
    TYPE: `Printed on:`
    PRESS: Space Bar once
    SELECT: Date button (as labeled in Figure 2.20)
    CLICK: OK command button
    You will see the custom header appear in the Page Setup dialog box.

9. To select a predefined footer:
   SELECT: Page 1 from the Footer drop-down list box

10. To specify the area of the workbook that you want printed:
    SELECT: Sheet tab
    The Page Setup dialog box appears as shown in Figure 2.21.

Figure 2.21

Page Setup dialog
box: Sheet tab

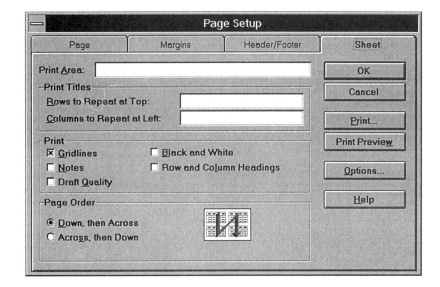

11. To select the Print Area text box, position the I-beam mouse pointer anywhere in the text box and click once.

12. TYPE: a1:h9
    (*Note*: You may find it easier to select the range of cells you want to print prior to entering the Page Setup dialog box.)

13. For this example, we do not want to print gridlines or row and column headings along with the worksheet. Therefore, make sure that there are no check boxes selected in the Print group before proceeding.

14. To complete the Page Setup dialog box and return to the worksheet:
    PRESS: (Enter) or CLICK: OK

Quick Reference	1.	CHOOSE: File, Page Setup
Specifying Page	2.	SELECT: Page tab to specify print orientation and paper size
Layout Settings	3.	SELECT: Margins tab to specify left, right, top, and bottom margins
	4.	SELECT: Header/Footer tab to specify a header and footer
	5.	SELECT: Sheet tab to specify the area to print and other options
	6.	PRESS: Enter or CLICK: OK

PREVIEWING THE OUTPUT

You can preview a workbook in a full-page display using the File, Print Preview command or the Print Preview button (⬛). Once the preview is displayed, use the Next and Previous buttons near the top of the screen to move through the document page by page. Notice that the mouse pointer changes to a magnifying glass over the page display area to allow you to zoom in on a portion of the page. You click once to zoom in and click a second time to zoom out. If you need to modify some page layout options, you can click the Setup button to display the Page Setup dialog box or the Margins button to drag margin lines right in the Preview window.

Perform the following steps.

1. To preview the SALES94 workbook:
    CHOOSE: File, Print Preview
    A full-page Preview window appears. (*Note*: You can also click the Print Preview button (⬛) to preview a worksheet.)

2. To zoom in on the page:
    CLICK: Zoom command button

3. Using the scroll bars, move the window so that your Preview window appears similar to Figure 2.22. You will notice that the date in the header differs from your date.

Figure 2.22

Print Preview display

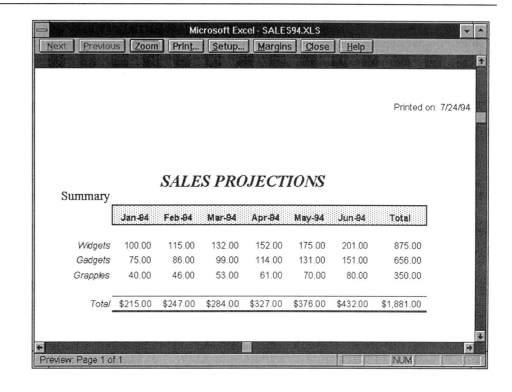

4. To zoom out:
   CLICK: Zoom button
   (*Note*: You can also click directly on the page using the mouse pointer to zoom in and out.)

5. When you are finished previewing the worksheet:
   PRESS: Esc or CLICK: Close

Quick Reference	1. CHOOSE: File, Print Preview
Previewing Your	2. SELECT: Zoom button to zoom in and out on a page
Worksheet	3. SELECT: Page Setup button to modify the page layout options
	4. SELECT: Margins button to modify the margin settings
	5. PRESS: Esc or CLICK: Close

PRINTING THE SELECTED RANGE

When you are satisfied with your worksheet in the Preview mode, choose File, Print or click the Print button (🖫) to send it to the printer. A dialog box appears with some final print options, as shown in Figure 2.23.

Figure 2.23

Print dialog box

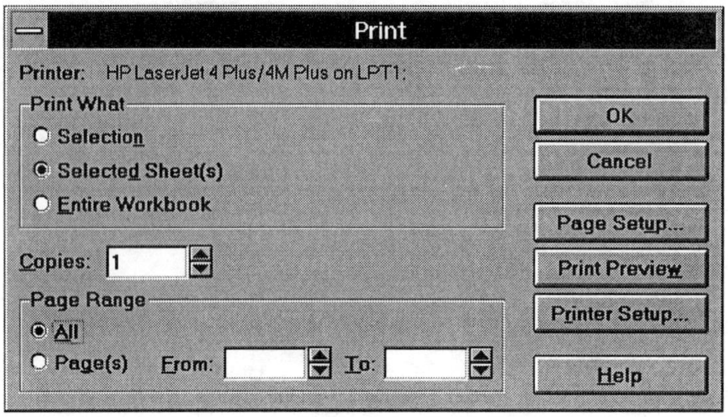

Perform the following steps to print your worksheet.

1. To send the worksheet to the printer without displaying the Print dialog box:
    CLICK: Print button (⬛)
    The document is printed using the default settings.

2. Save the worksheet as SALES94 to the Advantage Diskette and then exit Excel.

Quick Reference	1. CHOOSE: File, Print or CLICK: Print button (⬛)
Printing a	2. SELECT: additional print options, as desired
Worksheet	3. PRESS: [Enter] or CLICK: OK

SUMMARY

This session introduced you to the everyday procedures required to effectively work with Microsoft Excel. To try out these procedures, you created a workbook and practiced entering formulas and the SUM function. The majority of the session, however, dealt with Excel's formatting capabilities for producing presentation quality output. Column widths, row heights, fonts, numeric formats, cell alignments, borders, and shading were all modified in customizing the sample workbook. Toward the end of the session, you concentrated on setting up and previewing a workbook for printing.

Many of the commands introduced in the session are provided in Table 2.1, the Command Summary.

Table 2.1	*Command*	*Description*
Command Summary	Tools, Spelling	Spell-checks a cell range, worksheet, or a workbook.
	Format, Column, Width	Changes the column width.
	Format, Column, AutoFit Selection	Changes the column width to the best fit.
	Format, Row, Height	Changes the row height.
	Format, Cells	Font tab: Applies fonts, styles, and point sizes to cells. Number tab: Changes the appearance of values. Alignment tab: Changes the alignment of a cell. Borders tab: Applies borders to cells. Patterns tab: Applies shading to cells.
	Format, AutoFormat	Formats the selected range using predefined styles.
	Tools, Options	Removes gridlines from the screen display.
	Edit, Clear, Formats	Removes formatting from the selected cell range.
	File, Open	Opens an existing workbook file.
	File, Page Setup	Sets the print area, margins, headers, and footers.
	File, Print Preview	Previews the workbook before printing.
	File, Print	Prints the workbook.

KEY TERMS

cell alignment   In spreadsheets, the positioning of data entered into a cell in relation to the cell borders.

cell range   One or more cells in a spreadsheet that together form a rectangle.

column width   The width of a worksheet column measured in characters. Because the actual width of a group of characters changes depending on the font size, it is often used only as a relative measure.

font   All the characters of one size in a particular *typeface*; includes numbers, punctuation marks, and upper- and lowercase letters.

footers   Descriptive information (such as page number and date) that appears at the bottom of each page of a document.

functions   Shortcuts that can be used in formulas to perform calculations.

gridlines   The lines on an Excel worksheet that assist the user in lining up the cell pointer with a particular column letter or row number.

headers   Descriptive information (such as page number and date) that appears at the top of each page of a document.

margins   Space between the edge of the paper and the right, left, top, and bottom edges of printed text.

Print Manager   A Windows program that intercepts print instructions from applications. The Print Manager uses a print queue to line up documents waiting for printer time.

print queue   In printing, a program that uses memory and the disk to line up and prioritize documents waiting for printer time.

row height   The height of a worksheet row measured in points. Points are the measurement unit for type—there are 72 points to the inch.

SUM function   Function used to add values stored in a range of spreadsheet cells.

typefaces   The shape and appearance of characters. There are two categories of typefaces: serif and sans serif. Serif type (for example, Times Roman) is more decorative, and some say easier to read, than sans serif type (for example, Helvetica).

EXERCISES

SHORT ANSWERS

1. What is the purpose of the SUM function?
2. What is meant by a "best fit" column width?
3. How do you apply formatting changes to an entire worksheet?
4. How do you select multiple cell ranges?
5. What does "#########" in a cell indicate?
6. Does turning the gridlines off for the screen display affect the way the document prints? Explain.
7. What are some common Font Styles available in the Font tab of the Format Cells dialog box?
8. Define the acronym WYSIWYG.
9. Name the tabs in the Page Setup dialog box.
10. What unit of measure is used to specify the margins' widths?

HANDS-ON

(*Note*: In the following exercises, save your workbooks onto and retrieve files from the Advantage Diskette.)

1. This exercise retrieves an existing workbook from the Advantage Diskette, edits the information, and saves the workbook under a new file name. You also send a copy of the updated file to the printer.
   a. Open the QTR1 worksheet located on the Advantage Diskette.
   b. Modify the worksheet to reflect the second quarter's expenses by editing the cells listed below.

Move to Cell	*TYPE:*
D1	(your name)
B2	Apr-94
C2	May-94
D2	Jun-94
B6	43.44
C4	39.65
C7	119
D6	83.91
D8	98.60

c. Save this workbook to the Advantage Diskette under the name QTR2. (*Hint*: You should use the File, Save As command).
d. Specify a header that prints the current date at the top left-hand corner of the page.
e. Specify a footer that prints the page number at the bottom right-hand corner of the page.
f. Review the worksheet in Preview mode.
g. Return to the Page Setup dialog box and make the necessary changes to not print gridlines.
h. Review the workbook in Preview mode.
i. Print the workbook.
j. Save the workbook again to the Advantage Diskette and replace the old version of the QTR2 file.

2. This exercise uses the formatting commands covered in this session to enhance the QTR2 workbook.
  a. If the workbook is not already loaded into memory, open the QTR2 workbook located on the Advantage Diskette.
  b. Make the following changes to column widths:

Column	Width
A	15
B	10
C	10
D	10
E	12

  c. Make the following changes to row heights:

Row	Height
1	25
2	20
3	6
9	6
10	18

  d. Make the headings from cell B2 to E2 bold and italic.
  e. Center the headings over their appropriate columns.
  f. Make the Expense items (the row labels) from A4 to A10 bold.
  g. Right align the Expense items.
  h. Increase the size of the font for the title (in cell A1) to 18 points.
  i. Select the cells from B2 to E2.

j. Place an outline border around these cells and then shade the interior.
k. Change the screen display by removing the column and row headings and the gridlines.
l. Delete the word "Type" in cell A2.
m. Save the workbook as QTR2A to the Advantage Diskette.
n. Print the workbook.
o. Close the workbook.

3. This exercise provides a step-by-step approach for using the formatting commands covered in this session to create a memo or fax form.
    a. Open a new workbook.
    b. Move to cell A1.
    c. TYPE: Memorandum
    d. Center the title between columns A and E using the appropriate toolbar button.
    e. Choose an interesting font with boldface and a point size of 24 for the title.
    f. Make columns A through E 12 characters wide.
    g. Enter the following information:

Move to cell	TYPE:
A3	DATE:
A5	TO:
A7	FROM:
A9	SUBJECT:
C7	*your name*

    h. Right-align, italicize, and make bold each of the row headings in column A.
    i. Shade the cell range from A1 to E1.
    j. Shade the cell range from A11 to E11.
    k. Save this workbook as MEMO to the Advantage Diskette. Your worksheet should appear similar to Figure 2.24.
    l. Print the workbook.
    m. Close the workbook and exit Excel.

Figure 2.24

MEMO worksheet

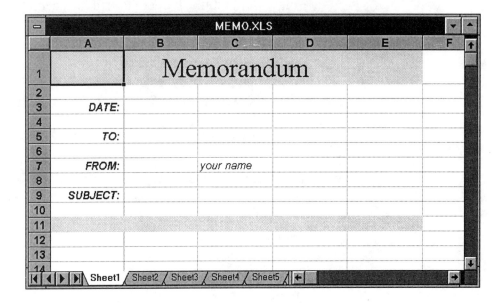

MICROSOFT EXCEL 5.0: INCREASING YOUR PRODUCTIVITY

Electronic spreadsheets are timesavers compared to the old pencil-and-paper spreadsheets. Now let us demonstrate some timesavers for the timesaver. Instead of entering the contents of every cell individually, as was done in the last session, you can use some command shortcuts that work with cell ranges. You can also use several built-in functions that provide powerful problem-solving capabilities.

PREVIEW

When you have completed this session, you will be able to:

Understand absolute and relative cell references.

•

Copy and move information using Excel's drag and drop feature and the Windows Clipboard.

•

Use special commands for copying formulas.

•

Use the AutoFill feature to create a series.

•

Insert and delete new columns and rows.

•

Describe the Excel built-in functions.

•

Use the following statistical, financial, and miscellaneous functions: SUM, AVERAGE, MAX, MIN, PV, FV, NPV, IRR, PMT, NOW, ABS, ROUND, and IF.

SESSION OUTLINE

Why This Session Is Important
Absolute and Relative Cell Addresses
Copying and Moving Information
      Using Copy, Cut, and Paste
      Using Drag and Drop
      Using Fill Right and Fill Down
Creating a Series with AutoFill
Inserting and Deleting Rows and Columns
Functions
      Creating Range Names
      Using Statistical Functions
      Using Financial Functions
      Using Miscellaneous Functions
Using Goal Seek
Circular References: Avoiding Them
Summary
      Command Summary
Key Terms
Exercises
      Short Answer
      Hands-On

WHY THIS SESSION IS IMPORTANT

Although the commands and procedures that you have used to this point in the guide are entirely correct, there are ways to improve your productivity in creating and editing worksheets. This session discusses copying and moving information and inserting and deleting columns and rows. It also introduces a variety of built-in functions that are available in Excel. The information contained here is vital to your efficient use of a spreadsheet.

Before proceeding, make sure the following are true:

1. You have loaded Microsoft Windows and Excel.
2. You have an empty workbook displayed onscreen.
3. Your Advantage Diskette is inserted into the drive. You save your work onto the diskette and retrieve files that have been created for you.

ABSOLUTE AND RELATIVE CELL ADDRESSES

This section adds a new twist to referencing cells in formulas. In previous sessions, you typed the cell address or clicked on the cell that you wanted to include in a formula. You should be aware, however, that there are two types of cell addresses that can be entered into formulas: relative and absolute. The differences between the two become important when you start copying and moving information in your worksheet.

When a formula is copied from one location to another, Excel analyzes both the original cell containing the formula and the destination cell. Excel automatically adjusts the cell references in the copied formula to reflect their new location in the worksheet. This adjustment spares you from having to type many similar formulas into the worksheet and thus saves a tremendous amount of time. A cell reference that adjusts when it is copied is referred to as a **relative cell address**. On the other hand, there are times when you don't want a cell reference to automatically adjust when it is copied. A cell reference that refers to an exact location on the worksheet and does not adjust is called an **absolute cell address**.

In Excel, formulas are entered using relative cell references unless you specify otherwise. To use an absolute cell reference, you must precede the column letter and the row number of the cell address with a dollar sign.

For example, to make cell B5 an absolute cell reference in a formula, you would type dollar signs before the B and before the 5, such as B5. If you wanted to have the cell reference automatically adjust the row number when it was copied but not the column letter, then you would type a dollar sign only before the column letter, such as $B5.

You will practice using these types of cell references in the next section on copying and moving worksheet information.

COPYING AND MOVING INFORMATION

To efficiently construct a worksheet, you need tools that reduce the number of repetitive entries that you are required to make. For example, once you have created a formula that adds figures in one column, why not copy that formula to sum the adjacent column as well? Two of the most common editing activities in a worksheet are copying and moving data.

USING COPY, CUT, AND PASTE

Excel uses the **Clipboard**, a Windows utility program, to copy and move data within the application and among applications. To place a copy of cell information onto the Clipboard in memory, you can use the Edit, Copy command, click the Copy button (⧉) on the Standard toolbar, or press Ctrl+c. To move cell information from the worksheet to the Clipboard, you use the Edit, Cut command, click the Cut button (✂), or press Ctrl+x. Once in memory, you can paste the Clipboard's contents by choosing the Edit, Paste command, by clicking the Paste button (📋), or by pressing Ctrl+v or Enter.

To practice using the Clipboard to copy information, you will retrieve the XYZCOPY workbook (Figure 3.1). This workbook provides an incomplete sales summary for XYZ Corporation.

Figure 3.1

XYZCOPY
workbook

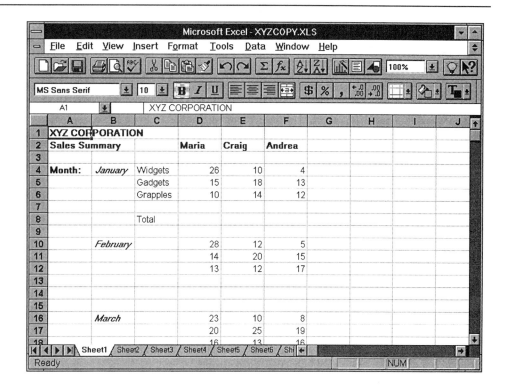

Perform the following steps to copy information using the Clipboard.

1. Ensure that the Advantage Diskette is placed into the drive.

2. To open the XYZCOPY workbook:
   CLICK: Open button (📂)
   SELECT: a: from the Drives list box
   SELECT: XYZCOPY.XLS from the File Name list box
   PRESS: (Enter) or CLICK: OK
   (*Note*: You can also double-click the file in the File Name list box.)

3. After the XYZCOPY file is loaded into memory, the first step is to sum the January data for each salesperson. Move the cell pointer to cell D8.

4. For the remainder of this session, let's cancel Excel's option for moving the cell pointer down one row each time you press (Enter):
   CHOOSE: Tools, Options
   SELECT: Edit tab
   SELECT: Move Selection after Enter check box so that no × appears
   PRESS: (Enter) or CLICK: OK

4. TYPE: =d4+d5+d6
    PRESS: [Enter]
    The cell should now include the sum of the figures in column D (51).

5. Take a copy of the formula and place it on the Clipboard:
    CLICK: Copy button (📋)
    A dashed marquee now surrounds the cell range.

6. SELECT: cell E8

7. Place a copy of the Clipboard's contents into the cell:
    PRESS: [Enter]
    Notice that the result of the formula is the sum of the figures in column
    E (42). Because the formula uses relative cell addresses, the formula's
    cell references automatically adjusted to the new column in which they
    were placed. Look in the Formula bar to see the new formula.

8. To see the effect of using absolute cell references, you are now going
    to edit the formula in cell E8:
    DOUBLE-CLICK: cell E8
    You will see the formula appear in the cell ready for editing.

9. PRESS: [Home]
    PRESS: [→] once
    The cursor appears to the right of the equal sign in the Formula bar.

10. To make a cell address absolute, you could type a dollar sign in front
    of the column letter and row number. However, there is a shortcut
    method, as demonstrated below:
    PRESS: [F4] (Absolute key)
    PRESS: [→]
    PRESS: [F4] (Absolute key)
    PRESS: [→]
    PRESS: [F4] (Absolute key)
    PRESS: [Enter]

11. Take a copy of the formula and place it on the Clipboard:
    PRESS: [Ctrl]+c

12. SELECT: cell F8

13. Place a copy of the Clipboard's contents into the cell:
    CLICK: Paste button (🖿)
    Notice that the result of the formula is still the sum of the figures in column E. The formula did not automatically adjust because it uses absolute cell references.

14. To clean up the Total line, you are going to enter a new formula and copy it to columns E and F. To begin:
    SELECT: cell D8

15. PRESS: [Delete]

16. TYPE: =sum(d4:d6)
    PRESS: [Enter]

17. CHOOSE: Edit, Copy

18. To paste the information:
    SELECT: cell range from E8 to F8
    PRESS: [Enter]

19. To move the Total line up one row so that it rests directly underneath the Grapples entry, you must first select the cell range:
    SELECT: cell range from C8 to F8

20. CHOOSE: Edit, Cut
    SELECT: cell C7
    PRESS: [Enter]

Quick Reference	1. SELECT: a cell or cell range
Copying and	2. To copy or move information:
Moving Cell	CHOOSE: Edit, Copy or CLICK: Copy button (🖿)
Information	CHOOSE: Edit, Cut or CLICK: Cut button (✂)
	3. SELECT: the destination cell or cell range
	4. CHOOSE: Edit, Paste or CLICK: Paste button (🖿)

USING DRAG AND DROP

One of Excel's most popular features is **drag and drop**. This method uses the mouse to drag selected cells around the worksheet without using the Clipboard. The drag and drop method is the easiest way to copy and move information short distances. The Clipboard is not used during a drag and drop operation; therefore, you can copy or move information only from one location to another. In other words, you cannot use drag and drop to perform multiple pastes. This method is extremely quick for simple copy and move operations.

Perform the following steps to practice using drag and drop.

1. To demonstrate how you can move cells using drag and drop:
   SELECT: cell range from C7 to F7

2. Position the mouse pointer over a border of the selected cell range until a white arrow appears.

3. CLICK: left mouse button and hold it down
   DRAG: mouse pointer downwards one row until a shaded outline appears around cells C8 to F8

4. Release the left mouse button. The contents of C7 to F7 are moved to the cell range C8 to F8.

5. To copy cells using drag and drop:
   SELECT: cell range from C4 to C8

6. Position the mouse pointer over a border of the selected cell range until a white arrow appears.

7. PRESS: ⌜Ctrl⌟ and hold it down
   CLICK: left mouse button and hold it down
   DRAG: mouse pointer downwards until a shaded outline appears around cells C10 to C14
   (*Note*: When you hold down the ⌜Ctrl⌟ key and click on the selected range's border, a plus sign appears at the tip of the mouse pointer.)

8. Release the left mouse button. Using the same process, copy the cell range from C10 to C14 to the cell range C16 to C20. Your screen should appear similar to Figure 3.2.

Figure 3.2

The XYZCOPY workbook after performing copy and move operations

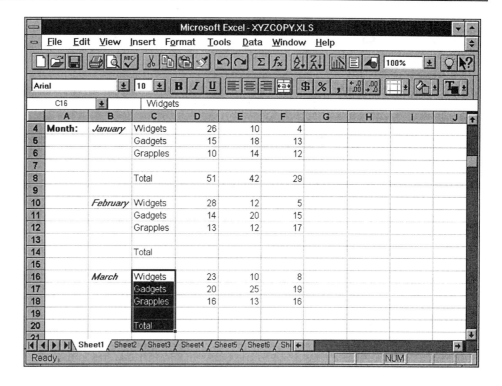

Quick Reference	
Move and Copy Cells Using Drag and Drop	1. SELECT: the cell or cell range to copy or move 2. Position the mouse pointer (a white arrow) over any border of the selected cells. 3. If copying the cells, press and hold down the [Ctrl] key. 4. DRAG: the selected cells to their destination 5. Release the mouse button and, if necessary, the [Ctrl] key.

USING FILL RIGHT AND FILL DOWN

Excel provides two commands specially designed for copying formulas: Edit, Fill, Right and Edit, Fill, Down. These commands are used when you have entered a single formula or function that needs to be extended across a row (Fill Right) or down a column (Fill Down). To demonstrate, perform the following steps.

1. Using the drag and drop method, copy the formula from D8 to D14.

2. To copy the formula in D14 to the cell range from E14 to F14:
   SELECT: cell range from D14 to F14 using the cross mouse pointer
   Notice that the cell with the formula appears in the top left-hand corner of the selected range.

3. To perform the copy:
   CHOOSE: Edit, Fill, Right
   The formula in cell D14 is immediately copied to the adjacent
   columns. (*Note*: The shortcut key for this command is Ctrl +r.)

4. SELECT: cell D14 only

5. To copy the formula in cell D14 to D20:
   PRESS: Ctrl +c
   SELECT: cell D20
   PRESS: Enter

6. To practice using the Edit, Fill, Right command:
   SELECT: cell range from D20 to F20

7. To execute the keyboard shortcut for the Fill Right command:
   PRESS: Ctrl +r

8. Save the worksheet as XYZDONE onto the Advantage Diskette.

Quick Reference *Using Fill Right and Fill Down*	1. SELECT: the cell that contains the information to copy 2. Extend the cell range downward or to the right, depending on where you want to place the copies. The cell to copy always appears in the top left-hand corner of the cell range. 3. CHOOSE: Edit, Fill, Right (Ctrl +r) or Edit, Fill, Down (Ctrl +d), depending on where you want to place the copies.

CREATING A SERIES WITH AUTOFILL

With Excel's AutoFill feature, you can quickly enter a series into a
worksheet. A **series** is simply a sequence of data that follows a pattern,
typically mathematical (1, 2, 3,...) or date (Jan, Feb, Mar,...). Although you
can use the Edit, Fill, Series command to perform some operations, Excel
provides the **fill handle** for entering frequently used series. The fill handle
appears as a black square in the lower right-hand corner of a cell or cell
range. Using the mouse, you drag the fill handle to create or extend a
series. You can also drag the fill handle of a cell to copy the cell's contents
to adjacent cells, similar to the Fill Right and Fill Down commands.

Perform the following steps to practice using AutoFill.

1. In this exercise, we move to a blank area of the worksheet to demonstrate some uses for the fill handle. To begin, do the following:
    CLICK: Name box in the Formula bar
    TYPE: a50
    PRESS: Enter or CLICK: OK

2. To enter a series of dates, let's move the cell pointer to cell B45.

3. TYPE: Jan
    PRESS: Enter
    Notice that you have to type in at least one cell entry as the starting point for a series. Make sure that your cell pointer remains on cell B45.

4. Position the mouse over the small black square in the bottom right-hand corner of cell B45. The mouse pointer changes to a cross hair.

5. CLICK: left mouse button and hold it down
    DRAG: the cell range outline to cell G45

6. Release the mouse button to complete the AutoFill operation. When the mouse button is released, the range is completed with the month headings Jan through Jun. Since Jan was the starting entry for the series, Excel increments the series by one month for each column.

7. Move to cell B46.

8. TYPE: Qtr1
    PRESS: Enter

9. DRAG: fill handle for B46 to cover the range from B46 to G46

10. Release the mouse button. Notice that Excel understands that the word "Qtr" refers to one in four. After Qtr4, Excel begins again with Qtr1.

11. Move to cell B47.

12. To create a custom data series:
    TYPE: Jan-94
    PRESS: →
    TYPE: Apr-94
    PRESS: Enter

13. SELECT: cell range from B47 to C47
    Make sure that both cells are selected before proceeding. Excel uses the two cells in the range to extrapolate the incrementing value for continuing the series.

14. DRAG: fill handle for C47 to cover the range to G47

15. Release the mouse button. Your worksheet should now appear similar to Figure 3.3.

Figure 3.3

Using the AutoFill feature to fill in a series of dates in the XYZDONE worksheet

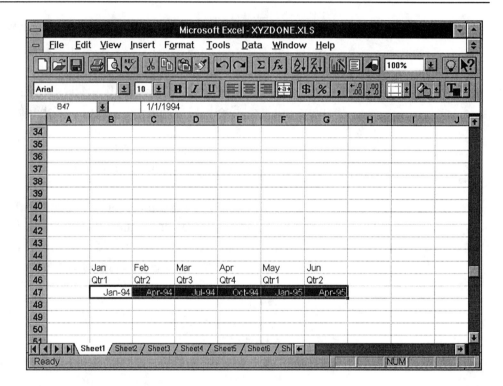

Quick Reference	1.	SELECT: the cell that contains the data to continue in a series
Using the AutoFill	2.	Position the mouse on the cell's fill handle, a small black square in the bottom right-hand corner of the cell, until it changes to a cross hair mouse pointer.
Feature	3.	DRAG: the fill handle to extend the series
	4.	Release the mouse button to complete the operation.

INSERTING AND DELETING ROWS AND COLUMNS

One method for quickly changing the layout of information in a worksheet is to add or delete rows and columns. As we mentioned in Session 1, people often create worksheets to solve a problem or design a report without fully understanding the entire situation. Therefore, worksheets must be able to evolve as the initial objectives become better defined and new needs arise. The ability to reorganize a worksheet by inserting and deleting rows and columns is an important part of this evolution.

To add a row or column to the worksheet, you choose the Insert, Rows or Insert, Columns command. To delete a row or column, you select a row or column and then choose the Edit, Delete command. The easiest method for selecting a row or column is to click its row number or column letter in the frame area.

Perform the following steps to practice manipulating rows and columns.

1. To view the top of the worksheet page:
    PRESS: Ctrl + Home

2. To add a blank column, you must first move the cell pointer to where you want the column inserted. (*Note*: Although the column location is important, you may select any row.) For this step:
    SELECT: cell E1

3. CHOOSE: Insert, Columns
    Notice that the new column is inserted and the original information is moved one column to the right.

4. To insert a column using the shortcut menu:
    CLICK: G in the column frame area to select the entire column
    The entire column is highlighted.

5. RIGHT-CLICK: any cell in the selected column
    CHOOSE: Insert
    The column is immediately inserted into the worksheet.

6. CLICK: B in the column frame area to select the entire column

7. To delete the entire column:
RIGHT-CLICK: any cell in the selected column
CHOOSE: Delete

8. To undo the last command issued:
CLICK: Undo button ()

9. To delete a row between the product figures and the total monthly sales line, you first select the row that you want to delete. For this step:
CLICK: 7 in the row frame area to select the entire row

10. To delete the entire row:
RIGHT-CLICK: any cell in the selected row
CHOOSE: Delete

11. To undo the last command issued:
CLICK: Undo button ()

12. Close the XYZDONE worksheet and do not save the changes.

Quick Reference *Inserting and Deleting Rows and Columns*	1. SELECT: row or column that you want to insert or delete by clicking the row number or column letter in the frame area 2. RIGHT-CLICK: any cell in the selected row or column 3. CHOOSE: Insert to insert a row or column CHOOSE: Delete to delete a row or column

FUNCTIONS

This section introduces you to some very useful functions that can save you a tremendous amount of time in creating worksheets. And don't let the word *function* conjure up visions of your last algebra or calculus class; Excel functions are substitutes for lengthy formulas and are often referred to as *electronic shortcuts*.

Excel provides a library of over 200 built-in functions to make entering complicated formulas as easy as possible. With the help of Excel's functions, anyone can calculate mortgage payments, car loans, and investment returns without ever having to take a finance course. Excel's functions are grouped together into categories: Database, Date & Time,

Financial, Information, Logical, Lookup & Reference, Math & Trig, Statistical, and Text.

A function is entered into a worksheet cell like any other formula. First, you type an equal sign followed by the function name. Depending on the type of function, you enter numbers, cell references, or range names within parentheses after the function name. Since you have already used cell ranges in the worksheet, the next section introduces you to creating range names. For step-by-step assistance, you can enter functions with the help of the Function Wizard. You simply click the Function Wizard button (f_x) on the Standard toolbar and answer the onscreen prompts.

CREATING RANGE NAMES

A **range name** is a label that you give to a group of cells on the worksheet. This label or name can be used in formulas and functions to refer to a cell or cell range. In other words, you can type =SUM(widgets) rather than =SUM(B3:B7). Not only is this easier for a person who is unfamiliar with your worksheet to understand, it also makes it easier to construct a worksheet.

To create a range name, select the cell range and then click once in the Name box in the Formula bar. When the information appears highlighted, type a name and press [Enter]. You can also click the down arrow adjacent to the Name box to display a drop-down list of all the named ranges in a workbook. This list is useful for entering range names into formulas and for moving quickly to a particular range.

Quick Reference *Naming a Cell* *Range*	1. SELECT: a cell or cell range to name 2. SELECT: Name box in the Formula bar 3. TYPE: a name for the selected range 4. PRESS: [Enter] or CLICK: OK

The following sections use range names in discussing some of the more commonly used statistical, financial, and miscellaneous functions.

USING STATISTICAL FUNCTIONS

Statistical functions are the most commonly used category of functions in spreadsheets. As described in Table 3.1, the SUM, AVERAGE, MAX, and MIN functions provide a great deal of flexibility and power for the typical application.

Table 3.1	*Function*	*Syntax*	*Description*
Statistical Functions	SUM	=SUM(range)	Adds together a range of cells.
	AVERAGE	=AVERAGE(range)	Determines the average value in a range of cells.
	MAX	=MAX(range)	Determines the maximum value in a range of cells.
	MIN	=MIN(range)	Determines the minimum value in a range of cells.

Perform the following steps to practice using statistical functions.

1. Retrieve the file named FUNCTION from the Advantage Diskette. This workbook file uses tabs to separate the exercises covered in the next few sections.

2. SELECT: Statistical tab
   (*Hint*: Using the mouse, click the worksheet tab at the bottom of the document window called Statistical.)

3. Before entering the functions appearing in Table 3.1, your first step is to assign a name to the range of cells containing the grades. To begin: SELECT: cell range from B3 to B12

4. CLICK: Name box in the Formula bar

5. TYPE: grades
   PRESS: [Enter]
   You can now reference these cells using the name GRADES.

6. SELECT: cell F4

7. To sum the column of results, use the SUM function:
   TYPE: =sum(grades)
   SELECT: cell F6
   (*Note*: You can enter the expression using lower- or uppercase letters.)

8. To average the column of results, use the AVERAGE function:
   TYPE: =average(grades)
   SELECT: cell F8

9. To enter the MAX function using the Function Wizard:
   TYPE: =max
   CLICK: Function Wizard (*fx*)
   TYPE: grades
   Your screen should now appear similar to Figure 3.4.

Figure 3.4

Function Wizard:
MAX Function

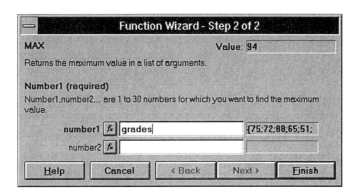

10. PRESS: (Enter) or CLICK: Finish

11. SELECT: cell F10

12. To find the minimum value in the column, use the MIN function:
    TYPE: =min(grades)
    SELECT: cell F12
    Your worksheet should now appear similar to Figure 3.5.

Figure 3.5

FUNCTION
workbook:
Statistical tab

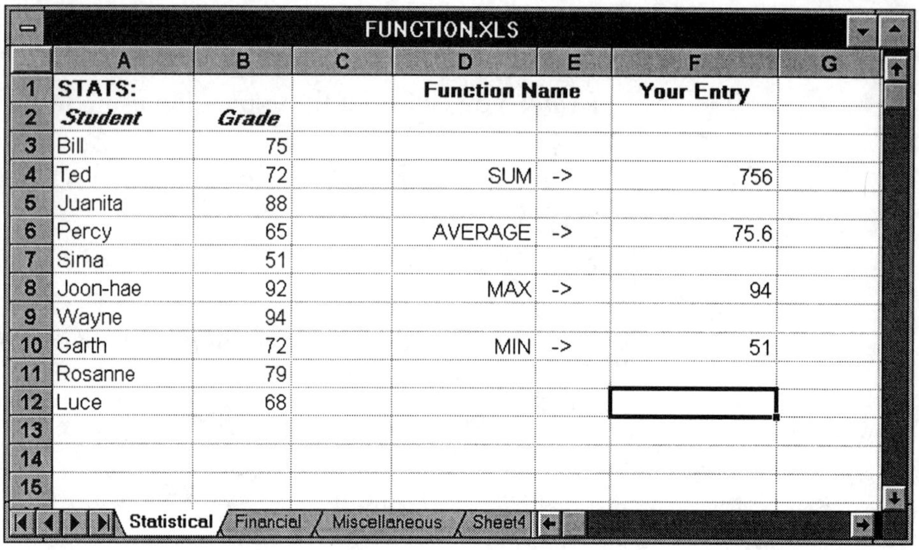

	A	B	C	D	E	F	G
1	STATS:			Function Name		Your Entry	
2	*Student*	*Grade*					
3	Bill	75					
4	Ted	72		SUM	->	756	
5	Juanita	88					
6	Percy	65		AVERAGE	->	75.6	
7	Sima	51					
8	Joon-hae	92		MAX	->	94	
9	Wayne	94					
10	Garth	72		MIN	->	51	
11	Rosanne	79					
12	Luce	68					
13							
14							
15							

Statistical / Financial / Miscellaneous / Sheet4

13. Change some of the numbers in the grades column (column B) to see the effects on the statistical functions.

14. Save the worksheet to the Advantage Diskette.

USING FINANCIAL FUNCTIONS

Excel's financial functions enable you to incorporate complex formulas into your workbooks. Some of the more popular financial functions, listed in Table 3.2, are devoted to solving investment decisions and **annuity** problems. An annuity is a series of equal cash payments over a given period of time, such as an investment contribution or a loan payment.

Table 3.2

Financial
Functions

Function	Syntax	Description
=PV	=PV(rate,periods,payment)	Calculates the **present value** (the principal) of a series of equal cash payments made at even periods in the future and at a constant interest rate.

Table 3.2 Continued	Function	Syntax	Description
	=FV	=FV(rate,periods,payment)	Calculates the **future value** of a series of equal cash payments made at even periods in the future and at a constant interest rate.
	=NPV	=NPV(rate,cell range)	Calculates the **net present value** of a series of investments and returns (cash flows) appearing in a cell range, given a constant discount or interest rate.
	=IRR	=IRR(cell range,guess)	Calculates the **internal rate of return** for a series of periodic investments and returns (cash flows) appearing in a cell range.
	=PMT	=PMT(rate,periods,pv)	Calculates the payment amount for a loan or mortgage, given a constant interest rate and number of periods.

Perform the following steps to practice using financial functions. The worksheet that you will use includes a loan payment calculation, an annuity, and an investment scenario.

1. SELECT: Financial tab in the FUNCTION workbook

2. SELECT: cell F3

3. As an example of a payment calculation, calculate the monthly payments for a $20,000 car loan. The payments are made over three years (36 periods) at an annual interest rate of 8.5%. In other words, the Present Value or PV for the calculation is 20000; the periods are 36 (3 years × 12 months); and the rate is 8.5%/12. The rate is divided by 12 months to change the annual interest rate to a monthly rate. Let's use the Function Wizard to help us enter this equation:
TYPE: =pmt
CLICK: Function Wizard button ([*fx*])
The Function Wizard dialog box appears for the PMT function.

4. DRAG: Title bar of the Function Wizard dialog box to move the window away from the figures in column B

5. With the insertion point in the rate text box:
    CLICK: cell B4 to place the cell address in the dialog box

6. Make sure that the rate is calculated on a monthly basis:
    TYPE: /12

7. SELECT: nper text box
    TYPE: b5
    SELECT: pv text box
    TYPE: b3
    Notice that the answer to the function already appears in the top right-hand corner. Your screen should appear similar to Figure 3.6.

Figure 3.6

Function Wizard:
PMT Function

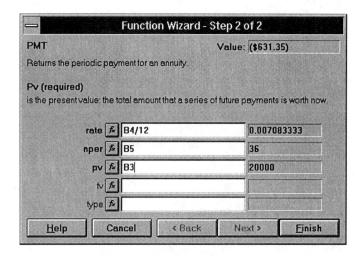

8. To complete using the Function Wizard:
    SELECT: Finish command button

9. To enter the function into the cell:
    PRESS: [Enter]
    The result of the calculation appears in parentheses to indicate it is a negative number, since the payment is a cash outflow from yourself to the bank.

10. SELECT: cell F8

11. If someone offered you a choice between receiving a flat $6,000 at the end of five years or an annuity of $1,000 per year for the next five years, with an interest rate of 8% per year, which would be the better offer? This problem requires a future value calculation:
    TYPE: `=fv(b9,b10,b8)`
    PRESS: [Enter]
    In this case, the better offer is $6,000 at the end of five years, since the future value of the annuity is only $5,866.60. With the majority of these calculations, you are concerned with the absolute or positive value for the number. Therefore, you can ignore the negative sign or parentheses.

12. SELECT: cell F9

13. If someone offered you a choice between receiving $4,000 today or an annuity of $1,000 per year for the next five years, with an interest rate of 8% per year, which would be the better offer? This problem requires a present value calculation:
    TYPE: `=pv(b9,b10,b8)`
    PRESS: [Enter]
    In this case, the better offer is $4,000 today, compared to receiving $3,992.71 in today's dollars over the next five years.

14. SELECT: cell F13

15. Some friends have an investment opportunity that they would like to share with you. The deal is simple. You give them $2,000 now and they will pay you $500 at the end of the first year, $1,200 in the second year, and $1,500 in the third year. In total, you are receiving $3,200 for your $2,000 investment. Is this a good investment? The net present value and internal rates of return are two profitability measures for such investments. To calculate the internal rate of return, you need to enter a guess of the expected rate of return. For this example, we use 20% in the function:
    TYPE: `=irr(b13:b16,20%)`
    PRESS: [Enter]
    The result for this calculation shows that you would make a 23.16% return on your investment.

16. SELECT: cell F14

17. Another test for the profitability of an investment is the net present value. We will use 10% as the expected discount or interest rate:
    TYPE: =npv(10%,b13:b16)
    PRESS: (Enter)
    An investment is profitable if the net present value result is a positive number. Your worksheet should now appear similar to Figure 3.7.

Figure 3.7

FUNCTION
workbook: Financial
tab

	A	B	C	D	E	F	G
2	*Loan Payments:*						
3	Loan Amount:	$20,000		PMT	->	($631.35)	
4	Interest Rate:	8.50%					
5	Periods:	36					
6							
7	*Annuities:*						
8	Payment:	$1,000		FV	->	($5,866.60)	
9	Interest Rate:	8%		PV	->	($3,992.71)	
10	Periods:	5					
11							
12	*Cash Flows:*	*Payments*					
13	0	-2000		IRR	->	23.16%	
14	1	500		NPV	->	$521.14	
15	2	1200					
16	3	1500					

FUNCTION.XLS — Statistical \ Financial / Miscellaneous / Sheet4

18. Change some numbers in the loan payments, savings account, and cash flow sections to see their effects on the functions. For example, what would the monthly payment be for a $15,000 car loan over four years?

USING MISCELLANEOUS FUNCTIONS

This section describes some miscellaneous functions taken randomly from their formal categories. Although often considered an intermediate-to-advanced topic, the IF function is one of the most useful functions available. The IF function can read a value in a cell and make a decision to perform a calculation based on the cell's contents. Each function is explained in Table 3.3.

Table 3.3	*Function*	*Syntax*	*Description*
Miscellaneous Functions	=NOW	=NOW( )	Provides the current date and time.
	=ABS	=ABS(cell)	Provides the **absolute value** of a cell.
	=ROUND	=ROUND(cell,digits)	Provides the **rounded value** of a cell to the number of digits specified.
	=IF	=IF(condition,true,false)	Performs a calculation based on the condition being met.

Perform the following steps.

1. SELECT: Miscellaneous tab in the FUNCTION workbook

2. SELECT: cell E3

3. TYPE: =now()
    PRESS: [Enter]
    (*Note*: You can format the date using the F<u>o</u>rmat, C<u>e</u>lls command.)

4. SELECT: cell E4

5. We want cell E4 to contain a commission rate that is based on the sales level. If sales are less than 10,000 units, the commission is 5%; otherwise, the commission is 6%. To enter the IF function:
    TYPE: =if(b4<10000,5%,6%)
    PRESS: [Enter]

6. To copy this expression to the next two cells:
    SELECT: cell range from E4 to E6
    CHOOSE: <u>E</u>dit, F<u>i</u>ll, <u>D</u>own

7. SELECT: cell E11

8. Let's enter the ROUND function:
    TYPE: =round(a11,2)
    PRESS: [Enter]
    (*Note*: Make sure that you type a11 and not the word "all.")

9. SELECT: cell E13

10. To get the absolute or positive value for the number in cell A13:
    TYPE: =abs(a13)
    PRESS: (Enter)
    Your worksheet should appear similar to Figure 3.8.

Figure 3.8

FUNCTION
workbook:
Miscellaneous tab

	A	B	C	D	E	F	G
					FUNCTION.XLS		
1	**MISC:**		**Function Name**		**Your Entry**		
2							
3	*Salesperson*	*Sales*			7/25/94 21:01		
4	Tom	15000	IF	->	6%		
5	Craig	7500	IF	->	5%		
6	Andrea	12000	IF	->	6%		
7							
8							
9	*Values for Functions*						
10							
11	449.5692		ROUND	->	449.57		
12							
13	-312.5		ABS	->	312.5		
14							
15							

Statistical / Financial \ **Miscellaneous** / Sheet4

11. Change some numbers in the worksheet to see the effect on the miscellaneous functions.

12. Save the workbook to the Advantage Diskette.

USING GOAL SEEK

Excel's Goal Seek command is a powerful "what-if" tool that lets you find questions for answers—like playing Jeopardy on television. For example, you can state exactly what you want to see as a bottom-line profit figure and Goal Seek automatically calculates the sales revenue required to meet this goal. How does Goal Seek accomplish this feat? Since profit is dependent on sales (sales less expenses equals profit), Goal Seek quickly substitutes values into the sales variable until the desired profit is achieved. For more complex problems, Excel provides the **Solver** tool which allows you to specify more than one variable to change in order to meet multiple goals and constraints.

To use Goal Seek, you choose the Tools, Goal Seek command from the menu. The dialog box in Figure 3.9 appears:

Figure 3.9

Goal Seek dialog box

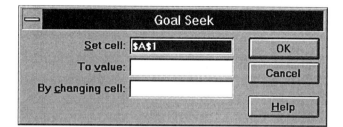

In this dialog box, you enter the cell that contains the formula for calculating the target value (for example, profit) and then enter the target value itself. You also need to tell Goal Seek what variable it is allowed to change in order to achieve this target value (for example, sales). Once completed, you press (Enter) or click on OK.

Perform the following steps.

1. SELECT: Financial tab in the FUNCTION workbook

2. SELECT: cell F3

3. Let's use Goal Seek to calculate the maximum loan amount that we can afford with monthly payments of $500. To use Goal Seek:
   CHOOSE: Tools, Goal Seek

4. In the Set cell text box, make sure that the cell address is F3.

5. To enter the monthly payment that we can afford:
   PRESS: (Tab) to move to the To value text box
   TYPE: -500
   Notice that we enter -500, since it is a cash outflow to the bank.

6. To specify the loan amount as the variable to change in this calculation:
   PRESS: (Tab) to move to the By changing cell text box
   TYPE: b3

7. To solve the equation:
   PRESS: [Enter] or CLICK: OK to accept the Goal Seek dialog box
   PRESS: [Enter] or CLICK: OK to bypass the Goal Seek Status
   When you return to the worksheet, notice that the Loan Amount has been changed to $15,839 in cell B3 and that the payment in cell F3 is now $500.

8. Close the workbook and do not save the changes.

Quick Reference *Using Goal Seek*	1. CHOOSE: Tools, Goal Seek 2. Specify the cell address of the formula or expression which contains the target value. 3. Enter the target value in the To value text box. 4. Specify the cell address of the variable to change. 5. PRESS: [Enter] or CLICK: OK

CIRCULAR REFERENCES: AVOIDING THEM

A **circular reference** occurs when a formula references itself in an expression. Formulas containing a circular reference produce erroneous results that can ripple throughout the entire worksheet. The problem with these formulas is that Excel cannot resolve the reference and therefore displays a zero in the cell. For example, in a few moments you will type a formula into cell A4 that is intended to add three amounts above it. However, you're going to type it in incorrectly and include a circular reference in the formula. The correct formula would be =SUM(A1:A3). You will type =SUM(A1:A4). When you finish typing the formula and press [Enter], Excel warns you that there is a circular reference. When you acknowledge Excel's warning, the Status bar at the bottom of the application window displays the cell in which the circular reference was discovered.

One of the best ways to understand circular references is to create one. In the steps below you will create a new workbook with a circular reference.

1. Open a new worksheet:
   CLICK: New button ([])

2. Enter the following information into the worksheet:

   Move to cell   *TYPE:*
      A1   10
      A2   12
      A3   20

3. SELECT: cell A4

4. In this cell you will enter an incorrect SUM function:
   TYPE: =sum(a1:a4)
   PRESS: [Enter]

5. A dialog box appears containing a warning message that your formula contains a circular reference. To accept the warning:
   PRESS: [Enter] or CLICK: OK
   Because Excel could not resolve the circular reference, the answer is displayed as 0. Notice that the Status bar at the bottom of the application window directs you to the cell that contains the circular reference. To eliminate the circular reference, you edit the cell that contains the formula with the circular reference—in this case, cell A4.

6. Close the worksheet and do not save the changes.

SUMMARY

This section explored several new formatting commands for changing the layout of your worksheet. After a discussion on relative and absolute cell addresses, you were introduced to the commands and shortcut keys for copying and moving information around your worksheet. Some final formatting commands were introduced for inserting and deleting columns and rows in your worksheet.

The latter half of the session introduced several of Excel's built-in functions. The Statistical and Financial categories were emphasized with the SUM, AVERAGE, MAX, MIN, PV, FV, IRR, NPV, and PMT functions. Several miscellaneous functions were also introduced, including the IF function for calculating an expression based on a set of conditions.

Many of the commands used in the session are provided in Table 3.4, the Command Summary. See Tables 3.1 to 3.3 for the Function summaries.

Table 3.4	*Command*	*Description*
Command Summary	Edit, Copy or (📋)	Places a copy of a cell or cell range onto the Clipboard.
	Edit, Cut or (✂)	Moves a cell or cell range from the worksheet to the Clipboard.
	Edit, Paste or (📋)	Pastes the contents of the Clipboard into the active cell or selected cell range.
	Edit, Fill, Right	Copies a cell to adjacent cells across the worksheet.
	Edit, Fill, Down	Copies a cell to adjacent cells down the worksheet.
	Insert, Column/Row	Inserts a column or row in the worksheet.
	Edit, Delete	Deletes a column or row from the worksheet.
	Tools, Goal Seek	Launches the Goal Seek tool for performing "what-if" analysis.

KEY TERMS

absolute cell address   Cell reference in an electronic spreadsheet program that does not adjust when copied to other cells.

absolute value   The value of a real number, disregarding its sign. For example, the absolute value of the number –5 is 5.

annuity   A series of equal cash payments over a given period of time.

circular reference   The situation created when a formula references its own cell address in an expression.

Clipboard In Windows, the Clipboard is a program that allows you to copy and move information within an application or among applications. The Clipboard temporarily stores the information in memory before you paste the data in a new location.

drag and drop A feature of Windows that allows you to copy and move information by dragging cell information from one location to another using the mouse.

fill handle The small black square that is located in the bottom right-hand corner of a cell or cell range. You use the fill handle to create a series or to copy cell information (similarly to the Edit, Fill, Right and Edit, Fill, Down commands).

future value The value in future dollars of a series of equal cash payments.

internal rate of return The rate of return at which the net present value is 0.

net present value A calculation used to determine whether an investment provides a positive or negative return, based on a series of cash outflows and inflows.

present value The value in present-day dollars of a series of equal cash payments made sometime in the future.

range name A name that is given to a range of cells in the worksheet. This name can then be used in formulas and functions to refer to the cell range.

relative cell address Cell reference in an electronic spreadsheet program that automatically adjusts when copied to other cells.

rounded value The value of a number rounded to a specific number of decimal places. For example, the number 2.378 rounded to a single decimal place returns the number 2.4.

series A sequence of numbers or dates that follows a mathematical or date pattern.

Solver An Excel tool that facilitates "what-if" analysis. Although similar to Goal Seek, Solver enables you to specify more than one variable to modify and more than one goal to attain.

EXERCISES

SHORT ANSWER

1. What is the difference between an absolute cell address and a relative cell address?
2. What is the primary difference between using the Edit, Copy command and the drag and drop method to copy information?
3. Explain the fastest way to put monthly headings at the top of your worksheet (i.e., January, February, March,...).
4. Why would you want to name a range of cells?
5. List the function categories in Excel.
6. Describe four statistical functions.
7. Describe five financial functions.
8. What is the purpose of the NOW function?
9. What is the purpose of the IF function?
10. What is a circular reference? How would you locate the cell that contains a circular reference?

HANDS-ON

(*Note*: In the following exercises, save your workbooks onto and retrieve files from the Advantage Diskette.)

1. The objective of this exercise is to create the workbook that appears in Figure 3.10, reorganize the layout, complete the formulas, and then practice copying and moving information.
    a. Type the text and numbers as displayed in Figure 3.10 into the appropriate cells. Make sure that you type your name into cell C1. (*Note*: Don't worry about the labels spilling over into the next column, as you will increase the column widths in step c.)

Figure 3.10

INCOME
worksheet

	A	B	C	D	E	F	G
1	INCOME STATEMENT		your name				
2		Jan	Feb	Mar	Total		
3	GROSS RECEIPTS	3200	1554	1980			
4	EXPENSES						
5	Accounting	213	101	321			
6	Advertising	132	223	46.76			
7	Telephone	250	301.5	199			
8	Travel	144.51	78.54	101.3			
9	TOTAL EXPENSES						
10	NET INCOME						
11							
12							
13							
14							
15							

Sheet1 / Sheet2 / Sheet3 / Sheet4 / Sheet5

b. Insert one row between each of the following: the INCOME STATEMENT line and the month headings, the month headings and the GROSS RECEIPTS line, the GROSS RECEIPTS line and the EXPENSES line, and finally, the TOTAL EXPENSES line and the NET INCOME line.

c. Set column A's width to 18 characters and columns B through E to 10 characters.

d. Center the month headings from B3 to E3.

e. Make the month headings bold and italic.

f. Center the row headings in cells A5 to A14.

g. Italicize the row headings.

h. Make the title in cell A1 bold and assign a font of 14 points in size.

i. Enter the SUM function in cell E5 to sum the GROSS RECEIPTS.

j. Copy the function in cell E5 to cells E8 through E12.

k. Use AutoSum to sum the expenses for each month.

l. Enter a formula into cell B14 that subtracts the TOTAL EXPENSES for January from the GROSS RECEIPTS.

m. Copy the formula from cell B14 to the cell range C14 to E14.

n. Select the cell range from B5 to E14.

o. Apply a numeric format to insert commas and two decimal places.

p. Select the cell range from B3 to E3.

q. Place a border around these cells and shade the interior.

r. Select the cell range from B12 to E12

s. Add top and bottom borderlines to this range.

t. Select the cell range from B14 to E14.

    u. Place a single line for the top border and a double line for the bottom border.

    v. Save the workbook as INCOME onto the Advantage Diskette.

2. This exercise takes the INCOME workbook, now saved on the Advantage Diskette, modifies the worksheet, applies names to cell ranges, and then incorporates some of the statistics functions.

    a. If it's not already displayed, open the INCOME workbook located on the Advantage Diskette.

    b. Insert a row between the Travel Expense item and the TOTAL EXPENSES line.

    c. Select the cell range from B5 to D5.

    d. Name this cell range "Receipts" using the Name box.

    e. Select the cell range from B8 to D8.

    f. Name this cell range "Accounting." Note that Excel already uses the row heading name, so you just have to press (Enter).

    g. Name the cell range from B9 to D9 "Advertising."

    h. Name the cell range from B10 to D10 "Telephone."

    i. Name the cell range from B11 to D11 "Travel."

    j. Name the cell range from B13 to D13 "Expenses."

    k. Move to cell F3.

    l. TYPE: Average

    m. Move to cell F5.

    n. To average the GROSS RECEIPTS:
        TYPE: =average(receipts)
        PRESS: (Enter)

    o. Complete the column as follows:

Move to cell	*TYPE:*
F8	=average(accounting)
F9	=average(advertising)
F10	=average(telephone)
F11	=average(travel)
F13	=average(expenses)

    p. Copy cell E15 to F15 using drag and drop.

    q. To copy the formatting characteristics of the cells in column E:
        SELECT: cell range from E3 to E15
        CLICK: Format Painter button (⬚)
        CLICK: cell F3 with Brush mouse pointer
        The formatting is automatically applied to the same rectangular shape of the cells that you copied. Your worksheet should now look similar to Figure 3.11.

Figure 3.11

Formatting the
INCOME
worksheet

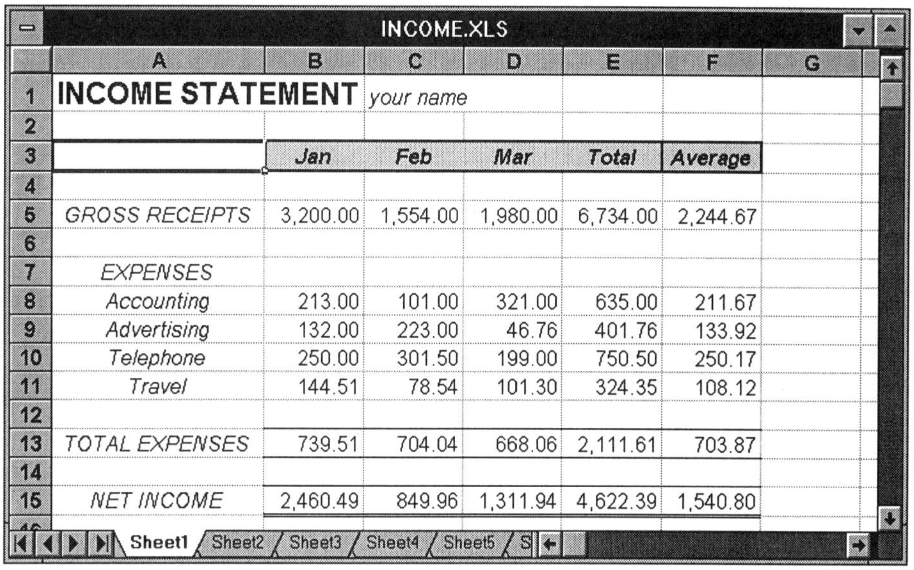

	A	B	C	D	E	F	G
1	**INCOME STATEMENT** *your name*						
2							
3		*Jan*	*Feb*	*Mar*	*Total*	*Average*	
4							
5	*GROSS RECEIPTS*	3,200.00	1,554.00	1,980.00	6,734.00	2,244.67	
6							
7	*EXPENSES*						
8	*Accounting*	213.00	101.00	321.00	635.00	211.67	
9	*Advertising*	132.00	223.00	46.76	401.76	133.92	
10	*Telephone*	250.00	301.50	199.00	750.50	250.17	
11	*Travel*	144.51	78.54	101.30	324.35	108.12	
12							
13	*TOTAL EXPENSES*	739.51	704.04	668.06	2,111.61	703.87	
14							
15	*NET INCOME*	2,460.49	849.96	1,311.94	4,622.39	1,540.80	

INCOME.XLS — Sheet1 / Sheet2 / Sheet3 / Sheet4 / Sheet5 / S

    r. Save your workbook as INCOME1 onto the Advantage Diskette.
    s. Print the workbook.
    t. Close the workbook.

3. This exercise creates a workbook for computing a mortgage table.
    a. To begin, ensure that you have an empty worksheet.
    b. Enter the textual information:

Move to cell	*TYPE:*
A1	MORTGAGE TABLE
D1	(your name)
A3	Principal Amount:
A4	Interest Rate:
A5	Years:
C4	Monthly Rate:
C5	Months:
C6	Payment:
A8	Payment #
B8	Principal
C8	Interest
D8	Balance

c. Change the column widths as follows:

Column	Width
A	18
B	15
C	15
D	15

d. Select the cell range from A3 to D8.
e. Right align the entire range.
f. Select the cell range from A8 to D8.
g. Use bold and italic for the range, and then apply an outline border with shading.
h. Enter the numeric information:

Move to cell	TYPE:
B3	150,000
B4	7.5%
B5	30
A9	0

i. Enter the formulas:

Move to cell	TYPE:
D4	=b4/12
D5	=b5*12
D6	=pmt(d4,d5,b3)
D9	=b3
A10	=a9+1

j. To calculate the amount of interest paid during each period (column C), move to cell C10 and enter the following:
TYPE: =d9*d4
PRESS: [Enter]
Note that the monthly interest rate is an absolute cell reference. Since the formula will be copied down the worksheet, enter the formula with an absolute reference to ensure that the expression always refers to cell D4.

k. To calculate the amount of principal paid during each period (column B), move to cell B10 and enter the following:
TYPE: =abs(d6)-c10
PRESS: [Enter]

Again, the formula will always refer to the total payment amount when copied, so an absolute cell address is used in the expression.

l. To calculate the amount of principal left (the Balance for column D), move to cell D10 and enter the following:

TYPE: =d9-b10

PRESS: (Enter)

m. Select the cell range from A10 to D10.

n. Format the numbers to appear with commas and no decimal places.

o. Select the cell range from A10 to D189.

p. CHOOSE: Edit, Fill, Down

q. Return to cell A1.

r. Change the loan principal amount from 150,000 to 175,000. Watch the worksheet recalculate the payments for each period.

s. Change the number of years to 25. Note the change in the ratio between the principal being paid back each period and the interest paid on the money borrowed.

t. Save the workbook as MORTGAGE onto the Advantage Diskette. Your worksheet should now look similar to Figure 3.12.

Figure 3.12

MORTGAGE worksheet

	A	B	C	D	E
			MORTGAGE.XLS		
1	MORTGAGE TABLE			*your name*	
2					
3	Principal Amount:	175,000			
4	Interest Rate:	7.50%	Monthly Rate:	0.00625	
5	Years:	25	Months:	300	
6			Payment:	($1,293.23)	
7					
8	**Payment #**	**Principal**	**Interest**	**Balance**	
9	0			175,000	
10	1	199	1,094	174,801	
11	2	201	1,093	174,600	
12	3	202	1,091	174,398	
13	4	203	1,090	174,195	
14	5	205	1,089	173,990	
15	6	206	1,087	173,784	
16	7	207	1,086	173,577	

Sheet1 / Sheet2 / Sheet3 / Sheet4 / Sheet5

u. Print the workbook.

v. Close the workbook.

w. Exit Excel.

MICROSOFT EXCEL 5.0: MANAGING A WORKBOOK

What you have done so far with spreadsheets is quite sophisticated. Now we show you how to use even more commands to manage your work: freezing titles on the screen, using windows to see different parts of a workbook, creating multiple-sheet files, consolidating worksheets and workbooks, and using macros to record and play back keystrokes. All of these features in Excel let you manage your workbooks more efficiently.

PREVIEW

When you have completed this session, you will be able to:

Freeze columns and rows as you scroll a worksheet.

•

View separate areas in a worksheet concurrently.

•

Consolidate information from several subsidiary worksheets into a summary worksheet.

•

Consolidate information from subsidiary workbook files into a summary workbook.

•

Create formulas that reference cells in other worksheets.

•

Describe what macros are and why they are important.

•

Create macros for use with all your worksheets.

Why This Session Is Important

This session introduces some techniques for working more efficiently with spreadsheets. Whereas the previous sessions concentrated on entering and formatting information in a worksheet, this session focuses on managing and withdrawing information. The techniques described in the following sections include using window panes to lock columns and rows on the screen, working with multiple windows, and using macros.

Also discussed in this session is the consolidation of data using formulas to link worksheets in a workbook and to link independent workbooks. This process makes it possible to store data in separate worksheets and then incorporate their data into a summary page. Without this capability, you would be required to store all the information relating to a particular application in one very large worksheet.

After constructing a worksheet, many people create macros to manage its daily use. A macro is a collection of keystrokes that can be played back at any time. Macros save you time and improve the reliability and consistency of your daily procedures. In this session, you will compose macros that you can use with any worksheet that you decide to create in the future.

Before proceeding, make sure the following are true:

1. You have loaded Microsoft Windows and Excel.
2. You have an empty workbook displayed onscreen.
3. Your Advantage Diskette is inserted into the drive. You save your work onto the diskette and retrieve files that have been created for you.

Freezing Titles

Most worksheets use row and column titles to serve as a frame of reference for information in the worksheet. Unfortunately, these titles often scroll off the screen as you move around the worksheet. Using the Window, Freeze Panes command, you can freeze specific rows and columns on the screen so that they appear at all times, regardless of where you move the cell pointer in the worksheet.

Perform the following steps.

1. Open the file named DAYS located on the Advantage Diskette.

2. SELECT: cell B5

3. To quickly move to the end of the row:
    PRESS: Ctrl + →
    The cell pointer moves to the end of the row, cell N5. Notice that you can no longer see the titles in column A—they have scrolled off the screen. Assuming that you do not memorize your worksheets, you would have to go back to column A to see what each row contained.

4. PRESS: Ctrl + Home
    The cell pointer moves back to cell A1.

5. By freezing the window **panes**, you can lock the employee names in the first column no matter how far you move to the right. First, you position the cell pointer below the row and to the right of the column that you want to freeze. For this step, move the cell pointer to cell B7.

6. CHOOSE: Window, Freeze Panes

7. Position the tip of the mouse pointer below the scroll box on the vertical scroll bar and click once to move down the worksheet. Notice that the worksheet window scrolls down but leaves the top six rows visible.

8. To move across the worksheet, position the tip of the mouse pointer to the right of the scroll box on the horizontal scroll bar and click once. Again, notice that the worksheet scrolls but leaves the leftmost column of employee names visible. Your worksheet should now look similar to Figure 4.1.

Figure 4.1

The DAYS worksheet divided into panes

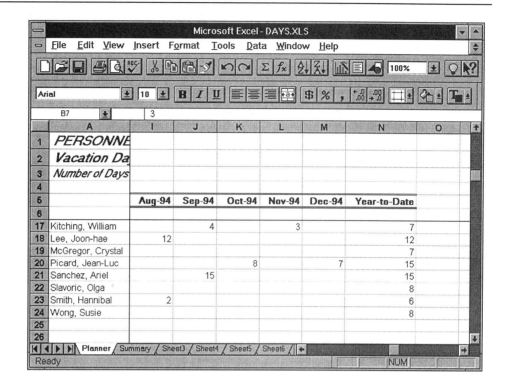

9. To return to your starting screen position:
   PRESS: Ctrl + Home

10. To unfreeze the panes:
    CHOOSE: Window, Unfreeze Panes

Quick Reference *Freezing Titles*	1. Position the cell pointer below and to the right of the row and column that you want to freeze.
	2. To freeze the horizontal and vertical worksheet panes: CHOOSE: Window, Freeze Panes
	3. To unfreeze the horizontal and vertical worksheet panes: CHOOSE: Window, Unfreeze Panes

When a worksheet is relatively large and is organized under stationary row and column titles, the Freeze Panes command for creating window panes is the right tool for managing your worksheet. However, a worksheet that is not divided into rows and columns requires another tool. The next two sections explore the process of dividing a worksheet's window into panes and creating additional windows for viewing the current workbook.

SPLITTING THE WINDOW INTO PANES

Similarly to freezing titles, you can manually split a worksheet's window into two or four panes which makes it easier to manage worksheets that cannot fit in a single window. You create the split by choosing the Window, Split command or by dragging the **horizontal split box** or **vertical split box** at the end of each scroll bar (both are shown below).

Horizontal Split Box

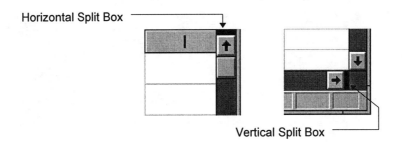

Vertical Split Box

Using the Split command, you position the cell pointer below or to the right of the column and row where you want the split to occur—as you would setting titles. If you prefer using the mouse, drag the split boxes to the desired window location. Once in place, you can finalize the positioning of panes by dragging the actual split bars that appear in the window. To move between two panes or among four panes, you simply click the mouse pointer in the desired pane.

Perform the following steps.

1. Position the mouse pointer over the horizontal split box until the pointer changes to a black horizontal double-line split by a two-headed arrow.

2. CLICK: left mouse button and hold it down
   DRAG: the split box downwards to split the window in half

3. Release the mouse button. Notice that you now have two vertical scroll bars for controlling both panes independently.

4. Position the tip of the mouse pointer below the scroll box on the bottom vertical scroll bar and click once to move down the worksheet.

5. Position the tip of the mouse pointer below the scroll box on the top vertical scroll bar and click twice to move the viewing area in the top pane. As opposed to freezing titles, you can change the viewing area in both panes.

6. Position the mouse pointer over the vertical split box until the pointer changes to a black vertical double line split by a two-headed arrow.

7. CLICK: left mouse button and hold it down
   DRAG: the split box to the left to split the window in half

8. Release the mouse button. Notice that you have divided the current worksheet window into four panes.

9. CLICK: *anywhere in the bottom left-hand window pane*
   PRESS: [Ctrl]+[Home]

10. CLICK: *anywhere in the bottom right-hand window pane*
    PRESS: [Ctrl]+[Home]

11. CLICK: *anywhere in the top right-hand window pane*
    PRESS: [Ctrl]+[Home]

12. CLICK: *anywhere in the top left-hand window pane*
    PRESS: [Ctrl]+[Home]
    This example demonstrates that you must click in the pane before moving the cell pointer in the pane. Your worksheet should now appear similar to Figure 4.2.

Figure 4.2

Dividing the worksheet's window into panes

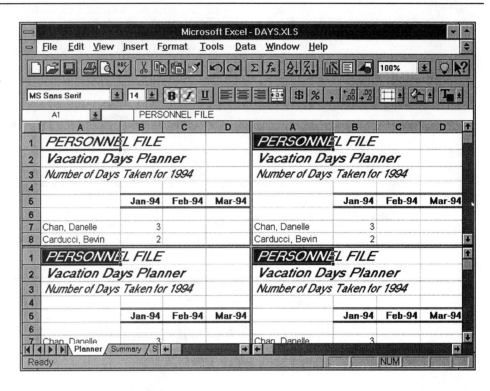

13. To quickly remove panes from the window:
    CHOOSE: Window, Remove Split

14. Close the worksheet and do not save the changes.

Quick Reference	• DRAG: horizontal and vertical scroll boxes to divide the current worksheet's window into two or four panes
Splitting the	
Window into Panes	• To remove panes from the current window:
	CHOOSE: Window, Remove Split

WORKING WITH MULTIPLE WINDOWS

Excel allows you to view multiple document windows at the same time. Each window may display different workbooks or provide different views of the same workbook. Multiple window views are useful when you have related information scattered in distant areas or across several worksheets in a large workbook, or perhaps stored in different workbooks. This section explains how to display and organize multiple windows in the Excel application window.

You can manipulate a document window using its Control menu (⬛) which appears as a small horizontal bar in the upper left-hand corner of the window. In addition to using the mouse, you access this menu by pressing **(Alt)**+Hyphen to move, size, or close the window. Before you can issue commands to affect a worksheet, its document window must first be active. You activate a window by clicking on it in the document area or by choosing its name from the Window pull-down menu. To close a document window, choose Close from its Control menu. You can also close a window by double-clicking its Control menu.

To automatically organize all the open windows in the document area, choose the Window, Arrange command to display the dialog box in Figure 4.3.

Figure 4.3

Arrange dialog box

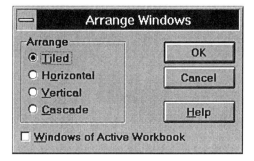

The Arrange dialog box offers several options for arranging windows in the document area. The Tiled option lets you maximize the space for each window in a pattern similar to floor tiles. The Horizontal option places each worksheet in a horizontal strip in the document area, while the Vertical option employs vertical strips. Once you have selected an option, you press **(Enter)** or click on OK.

Perform the following steps to practice working with multiple windows.

1. Before retrieving the DAYS workbook, close any worksheet windows, empty or otherwise, that are currently open:
PRESS: **(Shift)** and hold it down
CHOOSE: File, Close All and then release the **(Shift)** key
(*Note*: If there are no open windows in the document area, the Close All command does not appear on the File pull-down menu. In this case, proceed to the next step without making a menu selection.)

2. Open the file named DAYS located on the Advantage Diskette.

3. Let's practice working with document windows. A document window can be displayed as a window or it can be maximized to cover the entire document area. You can tell the difference by looking at the Title bar. If the name of the worksheet appears next to the words "Microsoft Excel" in the Application's Title bar, then the document window has been maximized. If the name of the worksheet appears in its own Title bar within the document area, then the worksheet is displayed as a window. In this step, you practice switching the DAYS worksheet between a windowed view and a maximized view.

    a. If the DAYS worksheet is currently maximized:
        CLICK: document window's Restore icon (‡)
        When a worksheet is maximized, the Restore icon is located on the second line in the top right-hand corner of the application window. (*CAUTION*: The Excel application window has Restore [‡], Maximize [▲], and Minimize [▼] icons also.)

    b. If the worksheet is currently windowed:
        CLICK: document window's Maximize icon (▲)
        (*Hint*: If you accidentally click the Minimize icon [▼], you can restore the document window by double-clicking the icon that appears at the bottom of the document area.)

    c. Practice changing the worksheet between a windowed view and a maximized view. Before proceeding, make sure that you have selected a windowed view.

4. Using the Arrange command, you can maximize a single window's size so that it covers the entire document area:
    CHOOSE: Window, Arrange
    SELECT: Tiled option button
    PRESS: Enter or CLICK: OK

5. To open a second window on this worksheet:
    CHOOSE: Window, New Window

6. The new document window appears over top of the original window. To view both windows at the same time:
    CHOOSE: Window, Arrange
    SELECT: Tiled option button
    PRESS: Enter or CLICK: OK
    Notice that the windows are identical, except for their Title bars. There are now two views of the DAYS worksheet: DAYS.XLS:1 and DAYS.XLS:2 (Figure 4.4).

Figure 4.4

The DAYS
worksheet with two
windows displayed

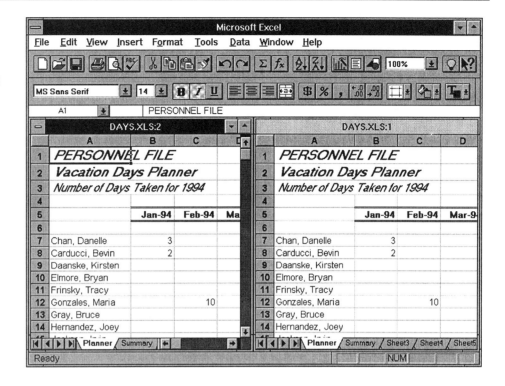

7. For a different window arrangement:
   CHOOSE: Window, Arrange
   SELECT: Horizontal option button
   PRESS: (Enter) or CLICK: OK

8. To change back to the vertical window arrangement:
   CHOOSE: Window, Arrange
   SELECT: Tiled option button
   PRESS: (Enter) or CLICK: OK
   (*Note*: With only two windows open, the Tiled and Vertical options
   produce identical results.)

9. Practice switching between the two open windows using a mouse:
   CLICK: *any part of a window in the document area to make it active*
   SELECT: *each open window several times*
   With the possibility of having multiple windows open in the document
   area, it is important to be able to switch among them efficiently. You
   can execute commands or type information only in the active window,
   which is set apart from the rest by its solid or dark Title bar.

10. To switch to a window that is covered by one or more windows, you use the menu command:
CHOOSE: Window, *window to make active*
After you choose the Window command from the Menu bar, the pull-down menu appears. At the bottom of this pull-down menu, a list of the currently open windows is displayed for easy selection. Practice moving between the two open windows using this command.

11. Make the first window active:
CHOOSE: Window, 1

12. PRESS: Ctrl + Home

13. Make the second window active:
CHOOSE: Window, 2

14. The DAYS workbook has a summary section located on the second worksheet file. To move to this worksheet:
CLICK: Summary tab (at the bottom of the document window)

15. Move back to the first window (DAYS.XLS:1).

16. SELECT: cell B7

17. In this step, you will change the number in cell B7 to see the effects of the change on the Summary section in the DAYS.XLS:2 window:
TYPE: 5
PRESS: Enter
The Average Vacation Days for Jan-94 changes from 3.00 to 3.67.

18. To test the limits of practicality for using multiple windows, open four more windows:
CHOOSE: Window, New Window four times

19. To arrange the windows in the document area:
CHOOSE: Window, Arrange
SELECT: Tiled option button
PRESS: Enter or CLICK: OK

20. Let's try the Vertical option in this step:
CHOOSE: Window, Arrange
SELECT: Vertical option button
PRESS: Enter or CLICK: OK
Your worksheet should now look similar to Figure 4.5.

Figure 4.5

The DAYS worksheet with six windows displayed

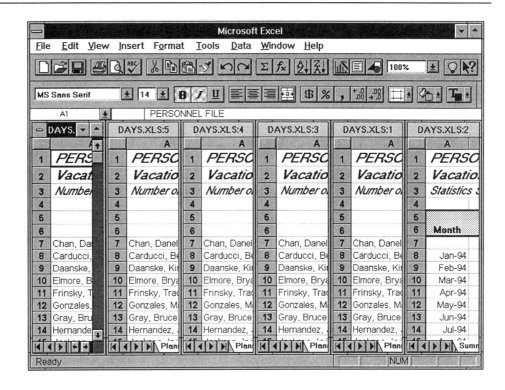

21. To clean up the document area:
    PRESS: (Shift) and hold it down
    CHOOSE: File, Close All
    SELECT: No when asked to save changes
    (*Note*: It is not necessary to use the File, Close All command in this exercise since you are closing only one file, DAYS.XLS. The Close All command is designed to close multiple workbook files that are open in the document area, as opposed to multiple window views.)

Quick Reference *Working with* *Document Windows*	• To create a new window view for the active worksheet: CHOOSE: Window, New Window • To arrange open windows in the document area: CHOOSE: Window, Arrange SELECT: *an option button, such as Tiled, Horizontal, or Vertical* PRESS: (Enter) or CLICK: OK • To close a window: DOUBLE-CLICK: its Control menu, or CHOOSE: Close from its Control menu

CREATING MULTIPLE-SHEET WORKBOOKS

In this section, you learn how to create and navigate a multiple-sheet workbook file. Multiple-sheet workbooks enable you to separate related information onto different pages in a single file. For example, imagine that you manage the advertising budgets for ten different brands of coffee. In addition to having individual reports for each brand, you need to produce a summary report that consolidates the budgets for the entire product line. Using a workbook, you can place the product summary report on the first worksheet and then each brand report on a subsequent worksheet. This three dimensional (3-D) capability enables you to easily manage and **consolidate** your information.

As a new feature in Version 5.0, Excel provides sheet tabs at the bottom of the document window. In a new workbook, Excel provides 16 worksheets by default. It may help you to think of a worksheet as a tear-off page on a notepad—the notepad representing the workbook. Although initially labeled Sheet1, Sheet2, and so on, you can enter descriptive names for each worksheet. You can choose any name up to 31 characters including spaces. However, you cannot use the asterisk (*), question mark (?), forward slash (/), backslash (\), or colon (:) in a worksheet's name. To move quickly to a particular worksheet, you scroll the tabs using the tab scroll buttons (shown below) and then click the desired sheet tab. You can also right-click any of the tab scroll buttons for a complete pop-up menu of the available worksheets and then make a selection from the menu list.

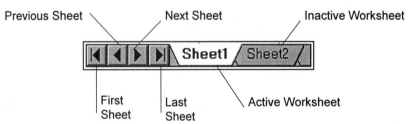

Excel's sheet tabs share the document window with the horizontal scroll bar. You can adjust how much room is devoted to each by dragging the tab split bar that is sandwiched between the two. Similarly to creating window panes using the vertical split bar, the mouse pointer changes to a black vertical double line split by a two-headed arrow when positioned properly over the bar. You drag the tab split bar back and forth to increase and decrease the share of real estate given to each component. If you are working in a single-worksheet workbook, you would normally drag the tab split bar to the far left to hide the remaining worksheets. In this section, you will practice navigating worksheets and executing simple commands.

Perform the following steps to create a multiple-sheet workbook.

1. The document area in the Excel application window should be empty. To create a new file:
CLICK: New Workbook button (▢)

2. To practice moving between the default worksheets:
CLICK: Sheet3 tab
CLICK: Sheet5 tab

3. To scroll the tabs to the right:
CLICK: Next Sheet button (▶) multiple times
Notice that the active worksheet, Sheet5, remains active (highlighted) as you scroll through the worksheet tabs.

4. To move to the last worksheet in the workbook:
CLICK: Last Sheet button (▶)
Although Sheet16 is now visible, Sheet5 is still the active worksheet.

5. To move to Sheet1:
CLICK: First Sheet button (◀)

6. To rename Sheet1:
DOUBLE-CLICK: Sheet1 tab
The Rename dialog box appears, as shown in Figure 4.6.

Figure 4.6

Renaming sheet
tabs in a workbook

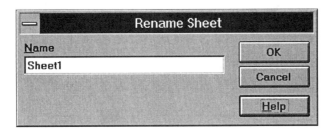

7. TYPE: Australia
PRESS: [Enter]

8. To rename Sheet2:
DOUBLE-CLICK: Sheet2 tab
TYPE: New Zealand
PRESS: [Enter]

9. Position the mouse pointer over the tab split bar until it changes to a black vertical double line split by a two-headed arrow.

10. DRAG: tab split bar to the left so that it rests to the right of the New Zealand tab (as shown below)

11. Although not so important with only two worksheets in the file, let's practice selecting a worksheet using the shortcut menu:
    RIGHT-CLICK: any one of the tab scroll buttons (◀◀, ◀, ▶, or ▶▶)
    Notice that the first two menu choices are the new tabs, Australia and New Zealand.

12. To move to the Australia worksheet:
    CHOOSE: Australia from the shortcut menu

13. To delete a worksheet in a workbook:
    RIGHT-CLICK: New Zealand tab
    CHOOSE: Delete from the shortcut menu
    PRESS: (Enter) or CLICK: OK
    The New Zealand worksheet is removed from the workbook.

14. To insert a worksheet between Australia and Sheet3:
    RIGHT-CLICK: Sheet3 tab
    CHOOSE: Insert
    The dialog box in Figure 4.7 appears.

Figure 4.7

Insert dialog box

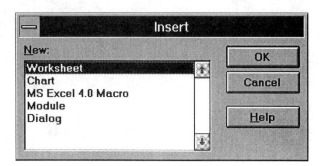

15. SELECT: Worksheet in the New list box
PRESS: [Enter] or CLICK: OK
A new sheet, called Sheet17, appears next to the Australia tab. You could double-click this tab and rename the worksheet to something more meaningful. However, we'll now proceed to the next section.

16. Close the workbook and do not save the changes.

Quick Reference	• Use the tab scroll buttons (⏮, ◀, ▶, or ⏭) to move through the available worksheets in a workbook file.
Working with a Multiple-sheet workbook	• Use the tab split bar to adjust the shared space for the sheet tabs and the horizontal scroll bar.
	• RIGHT-CLICK: any one of the tab scroll buttons to display a shortcut menu of all the sheet names
	• RIGHT-CLICK: a sheet tab to display a shortcut menu for manipulating (inserting and deleting) worksheets in a workbook

CONSOLIDATING YOUR WORK

Whether you need to combine revenues from several regions or calculate productivity statistics for several departments, Excel's consolidation tools allow you to better manage, organize, and present your information. In this section, you learn how to consolidate data using two methods. First, you use a single workbook file to summarize information. Second, you consolidate the results of individual workbooks to produce a new summary workbook. To begin our discussion, you are introduced to the Group mode for use with a multiple-sheet file.

USING GROUP MODE

In creating a workbook with multiple worksheets, the subsidiary sheets often have a similar, if not identical, layout to the primary or summary worksheet. Therefore, you can copy the layout of the first worksheet to the remaining subsidiary worksheets and then enter the specific figures for each. Excel provides the **Group mode** to assist you in creating identical subsidiary worksheets. When you select more than one sheet tab, Group mode is automatically turned on and all the commands that you issue affect all the selected worksheets. For example, Group mode enables you to change a column's width in one worksheet and have that same modification made to all worksheets in the file. To understand the effects of Group mode, we will format a multiple-sheet file.

Perform the following steps to practice using Group mode.

1. Close any workbooks that are currently open.

2. Open the SHIFTSUM workbook located on the Advantage Diskette. This workbook summarizes the production results for three shifts in a woodworking operation. The workbook file consists of four worksheets: one summary sheet and three detail sheets for each shift.

3. Let's start by naming the sheet tabs:
   DOUBLE-CLICK: Sheet1 tab
   TYPE: Summary
   PRESS: (Enter)

4. To name the Sheet2 tab:
   DOUBLE-CLICK: Sheet2 tab
   TYPE: Shift1
   PRESS: (Enter)

5. To name the Sheet3 tab:
   DOUBLE-CLICK: Sheet3 tab
   TYPE: Shift2
   PRESS: (Enter)

6. To name the Sheet4 tab:
   DOUBLE-CLICK: Sheet4 tab
   TYPE: Shift3
   PRESS: (Enter)

7. To select more than one worksheet at a time for Group mode:
   CLICK: Summary tab
   PRESS: (Ctrl) and hold it down
   CLICK: Shift1 tab
   CLICK: Shift2 tab
   CLICK: Shift3 tab
   Notice that all four sheet tabs are highlighted and the word "[Group]" appears in the Title bar.

8. Release the (Ctrl) key.

9. With Group mode turned on, you can issue commands in the first worksheet which will carry through to the last worksheet in the file. To begin, let's format the date headings to make them bold and italic:
SELECT: cell range from C4 to I4 on the Summary sheet

10. CLICK: Bold button (**B**)
CLICK: Italics button (*I*)
CLICK: Center button (≣)
These formatting commands are applied to all the sheets. (*CAUTION*: Although the Group mode feature is very handy, it can also be quite dangerous. Remember that you can see the effects of the command only on the current worksheet. Without realizing, you can easily erase or reformat information on other worksheets unintentionally. Be careful using this command!)

11. To turn Group mode off:
RIGHT-CLICK: Summary tab
CHOOSE: Ungroup Sheets
Notice that there is no longer the word "[Group]" in the Title bar.

12. Browse through the worksheets to see the effects of the last few steps:
CLICK: Shift1 tab
CLICK: Shift2 tab
CLICK: Shift3 tab
CLICK: Summary tab

Quick Reference *Turning Group* *Mode On and Off*	• To turn Group mode on, select multiple worksheets by clicking their tabs while holding down the Ctrl key. • To turn Group mode off, right-click any tab and then choose the Ungroup Sheets command from the shortcut menu.

CONSOLIDATING A MULTIPLE-SHEET WORKBOOK

With a multiple-sheet workbook, information in one sheet can automatically update information in another sheet. The SHIFTSUM workbook, for example, contains three subsidiary sheets for each shift. You will create formulas in this section that sum the values from each subsidiary worksheet into a summary worksheet. Thereafter, any changes to values in the subsidiary sheets are immediately reflected in the summary.

Perform the following steps.

1. Move to cell C5 in the Summary sheet.

2. As discussed in past sessions, you enter formulas by typing or pointing to cell addresses. To give you practice entering formulas, the following steps show you how to use several different methods for summarizing data. In a real-world application, however, you would create the first formula and then copy it to the remaining cells. To begin, enter a formula to sum the number of desks produced by all three shifts:
   TYPE: =Shift1!c5+Shift2!c5+Shift3!c5
   PRESS: (Enter)
   Notice that you separate the tab's name from the cell address with an exclamation mark (!).

4. Move to cell C6 in the Summary sheet.

5. You can also use 3-D ranges in Excel to specify a group of cells. To enter an SUM equation, do the following:
   TYPE: =sum(Shift1:Shift3!c6)
   PRESS: (Enter)
   An answer of 30 appears in the cell.

6. Move to cell C7 in the Summary sheet.

7. Let's create a formula by pointing to the cells:
   PRESS: =sum(
   CLICK: Shift1 tab
   CLICK: cell C7
   PRESS: (Shift) and hold it down
   CLICK: Shift3 tab
   TYPE:)
   PRESS: (Enter)

8. Move to cell C8 in the Summary sheet.

9. Let's perform the same procedure as shown in step 7:
    PRESS: =sum(
    CLICK: Shift1 tab
    CLICK: cell C8
    PRESS: (Shift) and hold it down
    CLICK: Shift3 tab
    TYPE:)
    PRESS: (Enter)

10. SELECT: the cell range from C5 through I8

11. To copy these formulas across the remainder of cells in the worksheet:
    CHOOSE: Edit, Fill, Right
    PRESS: (Ctrl)+(Home)
    Your worksheet should appear similar to Figure 4.8.

Figure 4.8

Consolidating a
multiple-sheet
workbook

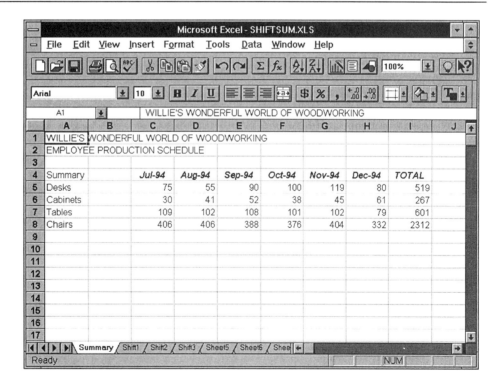

12. For practice, change some numbers in the subsidiary worksheets and
    then watch their effects on the summary worksheet.

13. Save the workbook to the Advantage Diskette under the same name,
    updating the old version of the file.

14.   Close the workbook.

CONSOLIDATING MULTIPLE WORKBOOKS

In addition to consolidating a multiple-sheet workbook, you can link
separate workbook files. Linking workbooks has two major advantages
over using one large workbook. First, the subsidiary workbooks are
smaller in size and therefore are easier to manage on a daily basis.
Second, subsidiary workbooks are not restricted to the same computer as
the summary workbook. For example, each department may control its
own workbook and submit the file once a month for consolidation. To
consolidate subsidiary workbooks, you open each file in the document
area and then, in a summary workbook, create formulas that reference cells
from the subsidiary workbooks.

Perform the following steps to consolidate information from multiple
workbook files. In this example, you compile three departmental
workbooks from XYZ Corporation into a single summary workbook.

1.   Close any workbook files that are currently open.

2.   Open the following files one at a time: XYZDEPT1, XYZDEPT2,
     XYZDEPT3, and XYZDEPTS.

3.   To organize the windows within the document area:
     CHOOSE: Window, Arrange
     SELECT: Tiled option button
     PRESS: [Enter] or CLICK: OK
     Your screen should now look like Figure 4.9.

Figure 4.9

Working with XYZ
Corporation's
departmental
workbooks

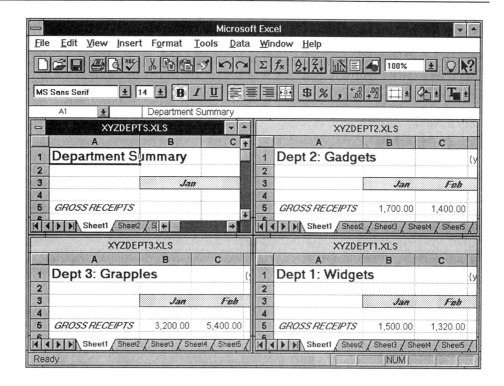

4. To move among the open windows in the document area, you position the mouse pointer on a visible part of the worksheet and click once. To practice, click the Title bars of the four worksheets. Notice that the solid or dark-colored Title bar represents the active worksheet window. When you are ready to proceed, ensure that the XYZDEPTS worksheet is the active worksheet.

5. Before you consolidate the XYZDEPT1, XYZDEPT2, and XYZDEPT3 worksheets into the XYZDEPTS summary worksheet, notice that the same worksheet structure and design layout were used for all the open worksheets. Although this is not necessary, it provides an instantaneous familiarity with each worksheet and makes entering the consolidation formulas much easier. To begin, you need to select a cell in XYZDEPTS to enter the first linking formula. Move to cell B5.

6. A formula that links subsidiary workbooks is entered the same as any other formula. To inform Excel that you are entering a formula:
    TYPE: =

7. CLICK: cell A1 of the XYZDEPT1 workbook to make it active

8. Using the scroll bars, move the worksheet window so cell B5 is visible and then do the following:
    SELECT: cell B5
    Notice the formula being constructed in the Formula bar.

9. To complete the formula:
    TYPE: +
    CLICK: cell A1 in the XYZDEPT2 workbook to make it active
    SELECT: cell B5
    TYPE: +
    CLICK: cell A1 in the XYZDEPT3 workbook to make it active
    SELECT: cell B5
    PRESS: (Enter)
    The summary worksheet calculates the answer 6,400.00.

10. Maximize the XYZDEPTS document window.

11. Before you can copy this formula to the other cells, you need to remove the absolute references to cell B5:
    DOUBLE-CLICK: cell B5

12. Use the arrow keys or the I-beam mouse pointer to highlight a dollar sign ($) and then press (Delete). Perform this step for each dollar sign that appears in the formula.

13. When finished editing the formula:
    PRESS: (Enter)

14. To copy the formula to the Clipboard:
    CLICK: Copy button (▣)

15. To paste the formula into all the remaining cells at the same time:
    SELECT: cell range from C5 to D5
    PRESS: (Ctrl) and hold it down
    SELECT: cell range from B8 to D11

16. Release the (Ctrl) key.

17. PRESS: (Enter)
    The formula is pasted to all the highlighted cells. Your worksheet should now appear similar to Figure 4.10.

Figure 4.10

Copying the consolidation formula to the remaining cells

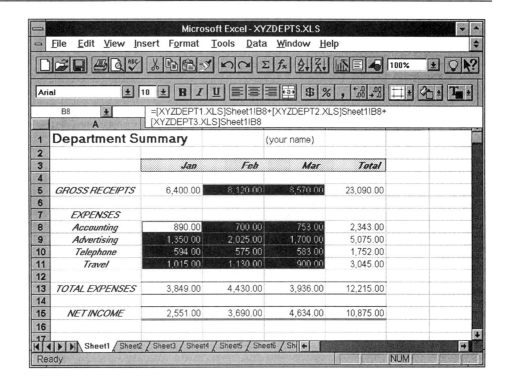

18. Save and then close each workbook.

(*Note*: Excel 5.0 includes a Consolidate command for consolidating worksheets. This command was not covered in this section because it introduces new concepts. The formula method for consolidating your workbooks is simply an extension of the skills you already possess. If you would like more information about the Consolidate command, please refer to the Microsoft Excel User's Guide that came with your software.)

WHAT IS A MACRO?

Many spreadsheet tasks are repetitive, such as enhancing titles with fonts and borders, formatting numbers, or printing cell ranges. To our benefit, Excel has assigned many of these monotonous tasks to toolbar buttons. However, there are still specific tasks that you may have to perform time and time again, such as entering and formatting your company name and address, that are not included as buttons on a toolbar. To save you time and improve the consistency of these operations, Excel enables you to store and play back keystrokes and commands in a **macro**. Using a special tool called the Macro Recorder, Excel writes the instructions for each task in Visual Basic, a Microsoft programming language. Using a macro, you can execute a series of instructions by pressing only two keys, clicking a toolbar button, or choosing a custom command from the Menu bar.

By incorporating macros into a worksheet, you make it easier to use for yourself and for others. Instead of having to remember all of the commands and keystrokes required to perform a procedure, you only have to remember a few simple keystrokes or which toolbar button to click. Furthermore, you can automate complicated tasks for co-workers or temporary personnel who are not familiar with using spreadsheets. If you are so inclined, you can even write your own Visual Basic code for creating menu commands, dialog boxes, and custom applications that don't even resemble Microsoft Excel.

CREATING MACROS

Macros are created by recording keystrokes or by directly typing in commands. In either case, the results are typically stored in a special sheet called a Visual Basic module. You can specify that macros be stored in the current workbook or in a special file called a **Personal Macro Workbook**. The Personal Macro Workbook is managed by Excel (you don't have to open or close this file) and provides a common area for storing macros that you will use with all your workbooks.

RECORDING A MACRO

The quickest method for creating a macro is to record the keystrokes that you press and the mouse clicks that you make while performing a procedure. Once recorded, the procedure may be executed again and again by selecting the macro. You turn on the Macro Recorder by choosing the Tools, Record Macro, Record New Macro command. When executed, the dialog box in Figure 4.11 appears.

Figure 4.11

Record New Macro
dialog box

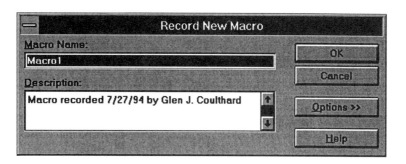

After entering a name for the macro, you press (Enter) or click on OK. With the recorder turned on, you perform the actions to be included in the procedure. Once finished, you turn off the recorder by clicking the Stop button (■) or by choosing the Tools, Record Macro, Stop Recording command. Excel automatically writes the macro for you and stores it on a Visual Basic module in the current workbook.

Perform the following steps to create a macro that automatically enters a company name and address and then formats the cell.

1. Close any worksheets that may be open in the document area.

2. Open a new worksheet:
    CLICK: New Workbook button (▯)

3. To create a macro you must first turn on the Macro Recorder:
    CHOOSE: Tools, Record Macro, Record New Macro
    The Record New Macro dialog box appears, as shown in Figure 4.11.

4. In the dialog box, type the name (without spaces) that you want to assign to the macro:
    TYPE: CompanyName
    PRESS: [Enter] or CLICK: OK
    Notice that the word "Recording" appears in the Status bar and that the Stop button (as shown below) floats above the application window.

5. As the first recorded step in the macro:
    PRESS: [Ctrl]+[Home]

6. Now, you can enter the company name and address information:
    TYPE: Sam's Superior Sailboats
    PRESS: [↓]
    TYPE: Suite 100, 2899 Seashore Drive
    PRESS: [↓]
    TYPE: Seattle, WA 98004
    PRESS: [Enter]

7. To format this information:
    SELECT: cell range from A1 to E3
    CLICK: Center Across Columns button (🔳)
    CLICK: Bold button (**B**)
    CLICK: Italics button (*I*)
    SELECT: Times New Roman from the Font drop-down list
    (Arial ±)
    SELECT: 14 from the Font Size drop-down list (10 ±)

8. To stop the recording:
    CLICK: Stop button (▪)
    And that's all there is to recording a macro! In the next section, you will get an opportunity to play back a macro.

Quick Reference	1. CHOOSE: <u>T</u>ools, <u>R</u>ecord, <u>R</u>ecord New Macro
Recording a Macro	2. Enter a name for the macro.
	3. PRESS: [Enter] or CLICK: OK
	4. Perform the procedure to be recorded.
	5. CLICK: Stop button (▪)

PLAYING BACK A MACRO

There are several methods for playing back a macro. You can execute a macro by selecting it from a dialog box, by pressing a keystroke combination, by clicking a toolbar button, or by selecting a custom command from the menu. In this section, you learn how to run macro from the Macro dialog box. For further information, please refer to the Visual Basic User's Guide that accompanies the Microsoft Excel software.

To practice playing back a macro, perform the following steps:

1. SELECT: Sheet2 tab

2. To enter the company name and address at the top of this worksheet:
    CHOOSE: Tools, Macro
    The dialog box in Figure 4.12 appears.

Figure 4.12

Macro dialog box

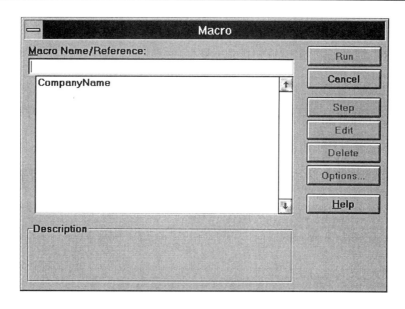

3. To run a macro from the Macro Name/Reference list box:
    SELECT: CompanyName macro
    PRESS: (Enter) or CLICK: Run
    The company information is automatically entered and formatted in the proper range of the worksheet.

Quick Reference	1.	CHOOSE: Tools, Macro
Playing Back a	2.	SELECT: the desired macro from the list box
Macro	3.	PRESS: Enter or CLICK: OK

REVIEWING YOUR MACROS

Since a macro is stored in a workbook, you can easily review and edit the Visual Basic code that Excel writes. In this section, you learn how to modify Excel's code and play back the new version of your macro. Perform the following steps.

1. To view the Visual Basic module:
   CLICK: Last Sheet button (▶|)
   CLICK: Module1 sheet tab
   Your screen should now appear similar to Figure 4.13.

Figure 4.13

Module1 sheet

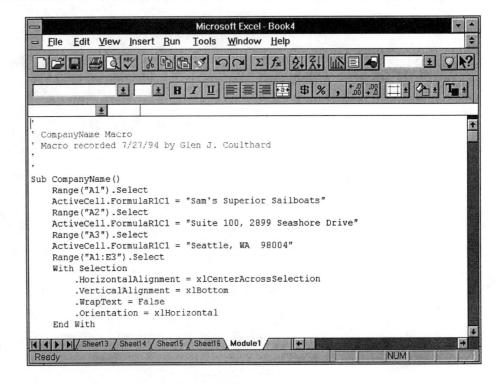

```
'
' CompanyName Macro
' Macro recorded 7/27/94 by Glen J. Coulthard
'
'
Sub CompanyName()
    Range("A1").Select
    ActiveCell.FormulaR1C1 = "Sam's Superior Sailboats"
    Range("A2").Select
    ActiveCell.FormulaR1C1 = "Suite 100, 2899 Seashore Drive"
    Range("A3").Select
    ActiveCell.FormulaR1C1 = "Seattle, WA  98004"
    Range("A1:E3").Select
    With Selection
        .HorizontalAlignment = xlCenterAcrossSelection
        .VerticalAlignment = xlBottom
        .WrapText = False
        .Orientation = xlHorizontal
    End With
```

2. You edit the Visual Basic code on this sheet as you would work with a word processing software program. For example, position the I-beam mouse pointer over the word "Suite" in the company's address. To select this text:
    DOUBLE-CLICK: Suite
    Make sure that the word is highlighted before proceeding.

3. Let's change the company address:
    TYPE: Room
    DOUBLE-CLICK: Drive
    TYPE: Road

4. To see the results of our editing:
    CLICK: First Sheet button (◄)
    CLICK: Sheet3 tab

5. To run the macro:
    CHOOSE: Tools, Macro
    DOUBLE-CLICK: CompanyName macro in the list box
    Notice that the new information is entered into the cells. This example demonstrates how quick and easy it is to edit the code created by Excel's Macro Recorder.

6. Save the workbook as MACROS to the Advantage Diskette.

7. Close the workbook.

Quick Reference	1. Select the sheet where your macro is stored, typically Module1.
Editing a Macro	2. Edit the Visual Basic code using basic wordprocessing keystrokes.

SUMMARY

This session introduced you to several commands and procedures that increase your efficiency and productivity when working in Excel. The first part of the session concentrated on dividing the document window into panes for freezing titles on the screen. This technique is useful when your worksheet is organized under static column and row headings. When your application consists of separate but related areas, separating the workbook into multiple window views helps you keep track of the workbook's relationships.

For consolidating detail worksheets or workbooks into a summary worksheet, the ability to organize and tile multiple windows in the document area is an incredible timesaver. The latter half of the session explored the use of macros in automating common tasks and procedures. Excel's easy-to-use Macro Recorder gives everyone the ability to create these great productivity tools.

The Command Summary in Table 4.1 provides a list of the commands and procedures covered in this session.

Table 4.1

Command Summary

Command	Description
Window, Freeze Panes	Lets you lock or freeze rows and columns on the screen so that they appear at all times.
Window, Unfreeze Panes	Unfreezes the area that has been locked using the Window, Freeze Panes command.
File, Close All	Closes all open documents in the document area.
Window, Split	Splits the window into horizontal and vertical panes at the cell pointer.
Window, Remove Split	Removes panes created by choosing Window, Split or by dragging the horizontal and vertical split boxes.
Window, New Window	Opens a new window in the document area for another view of the active workbook.
Window, Arrange	Arranges the open windows in the document area using square, horizontal, and vertical tiling options.
Tools, Record Macro, Record New Macro	Records keystrokes, commands, and procedures and saves them as a macro.
Tools, Record Macro, Stop Recording	Turns off the recorder to finish creating the macro; you can also click the Stop button (■).
Tools, Macro	Executes a macro using the menu.

KEY TERMS

consolidate   In spreadsheets, combining smaller worksheet files into a single summary worksheet. Consolidation procedures make it easier to manage large amounts of spreadsheet data.

Group mode   A special mode for working with multiple-sheet workbooks; enables you to perform commands on a single sheet and have those commands reflected in all other sheets in the file.

horizontal split box   A small box located at the top of the vertical scroll bar; used to divide a window into panes.

macro   A collection of keystrokes, commands, or procedures that can be executed using two keystrokes, a mouse click, or a menu selection. Macros are recorded or written by the user, saved to the disk, and then repeatedly used to perform frequent tasks or commands.

panes   When a document window has been divided into separate areas using the <u>W</u>indow, <u>F</u>reeze Panes command or the <u>W</u>indow, <u>S</u>plit command, these areas are called *window panes* or *panes*. A worksheet can have a maximum of four panes at any one time.

Personal Macro Workbook   A special workbook file, managed by Excel, for storing macros that you want made available to all your workbooks.

vertical split box   A small box located at the far right of the horizontal scroll bar in a document window; used to divide a window into panes.

EXERCISES

SHORT ANSWER

1. What is the main difference between freezing titles on a worksheet and dividing a window into panes?
2. What is the purpose of the <u>W</u>indow, <u>A</u>rrange command?
3. What are some advantages of linking workbooks?
4. What is the significance of a solid Title bar in a window?

5. How do you change the name of a sheet tab?
6. What is a macro?
7. How do you create a macro?
8. Where are the macros that you create stored?
9. How are macros commonly played back?
10. How can you view the macros that you have recorded?

HANDS-ON

(*Note*: In the following exercises, save your workbooks onto and retrieve files from the Advantage Diskette.)

1. In this exercise, you retrieve a workbook from the Advantage Diskette and practice freezing titles and viewing the worksheet using panes.
    a. Close all of the open windows in the document area.
    b. Open the CASH worksheet located on the Advantage Diskette. This worksheet is an incomplete cash disbursements journal. Make sure that you type your name into cell A3.
    c. SELECT: cell A8
    d. To see how many checks have been posted in the first quarter:
        PRESS: Ctrl + ↓
        Notice how the column text headings have scrolled out of view.
    e. Return to the top of the worksheet.
    f. Your objective is to freeze the titles in Rows 1 through 6 at the top of the screen. Then, when you move to the bottom of the column to enter new checks, you will still be able to see the column headings. The first step is to move to cell A8.
    g. CHOOSE: Window, Freeze Panes
    h. To enter more checks into the journal:
        PRESS: Ctrl + ↓
        The titles remain at the top of the screen as the cell pointer is repositioned at the bottom of the column.
    i. Enter the following checks into the journal:

Check	Date	Amount
51	17-Mar-94	550.45
52	24-Mar-94	300.00
53	31-Mar-94	750.25

Your worksheet should now appear similar to Figure 4.14.

Figure 4.14

CASH workbook

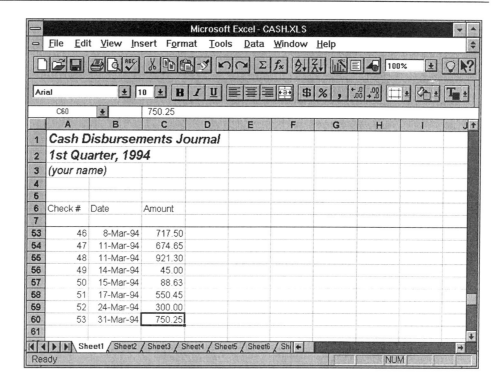

j. PRESS: [Ctrl]+[Home]
k. Unfreeze the row titles.
l. To create a new window onto the CASH workbook:
    CHOOSE: Window, New Window
m. Arrange the open windows horizontally in the document area.
n. Arrange the open windows vertically in the document area.
o. Close the window titled CASH.XLS:2 by double-clicking its Document Control menu.
p. Tile the single CASH.XLS window in the document area.
q. Save the workbook as CASH onto the Advantage Diskette. Replace the old version of the file.
r. Close the workbook.

2. This exercise practices consolidating separate subsidiary workbook files into a summary workbook. The company, XYZ Developments, is currently working on two projects. Each project has a project manager responsible for hiring subcontractors and consultants. Fortunately, XYZ's project managers are experienced in using Excel and have set up tracking workbooks. Your objective is to complete a summary

workbook that adds together the data from each project manager's file. (*Hint*: You will use linking formulas to consolidate these workbooks.)

a. Close all of the open windows in the document area.

b. Open the PROJECT1, PROJECT2, and PROJECTS workbooks located on the Advantage Diskette. Enter your name in cell E2 of the PROJECTS workbook.

c. Arrange the windows using the Tiled option.

d. Move to PROJECT1 and select cell B7.

e. Move to PROJECT2 and select cell B7.

f. Move to PROJECTS and select cell B7.
   The last three steps ensure that cell B7 is visible in each worksheet.

g. Construct a formula to add together data from the two workbooks:
   TYPE: =
   CLICK: PROJECT1 window
   SELECT: cell B7
   TYPE: +
   CLICK: PROJECT2 window
   SELECT: cell B7
   PRESS: Enter

h. Modify the cell addresses to contain relative cell addresses rather than absolute cell addresses.

i. Copy the formula in B7 to the cell range from B7 to M16.

j. PRESS: Ctrl + Home
   CLICK: cell B7
   Your screen should appear similar to Figure 4.15.

Figure 4.15

PROJECTS
workbook

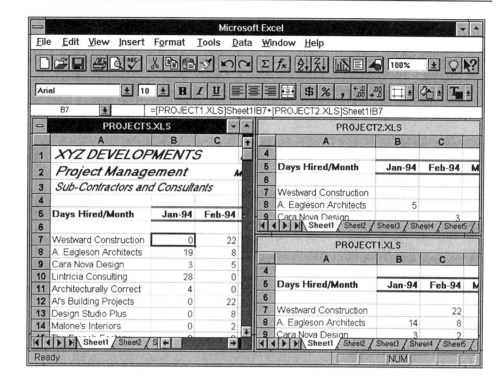

k. Save the workbook as PROJECTS onto the Advantage Diskette.
l. Close all of the open windows.

MICROSOFT EXCEL 5.0: CREATING CHARTS

Most business people recognize the benefit of using graphics to improve their effectiveness in delivering presentations. Clearly, a visual display is quicker in conveying information than rows and columns of tiny numbers. This session demonstrates how Excel produces visually stunning charts from basic worksheet information.

PREVIEW

When you have completed this session, you will be able to:

Explain the forms and principles of business graphics.

•

Describe the methods used to create charts with Excel.

•

Create a chart using the ChartWizard.

•

Choose from a variety of chart types and formats.

•

Customize a chart with titles, free-form text, legends, and arrows.

•

Save and print a chart.

Why This Session Is Important
Forms of Business Graphics
       Line Charts
       Bar or Column Charts
       Pie Charts
       Scatter Plot Charts
Principles of Business Graphics
       Simplicity
       Unity
       Emphasis
       Balance
Using Excel to Create Charts
Creating a Chart
       Charting a Single Range
       Charting Multiple Ranges
Working with Charts
Selecting a Chart Type
Customizing and Formatting a Chart
       Attaching Titles
       Adding a Legend
       Entering Free-Form Text
       Using Arrows for Emphasis
       Choosing Fonts and Patterns
Printing a Chart
Embedding a Chart
Summary
       Command Summary
Key Terms
Exercises
       Short Answer
       Hands-On

WHY THIS SESSION IS IMPORTANT

A graphic representation of worksheet data is far more effective than the numbers alone for the same reason that road maps are easier to follow than written directions. The majority of people are visual learners and seem to remember what they see better than what they hear or read. **Graphics**, which are the pictorial representation of words and data, provide us with a superior method of presentation.

Graphics are produced in a variety of formats to suit the specific needs of the business professional. For example, microcomputer images can be displayed on a monitor, photographed, plotted on paper (black and white or color), or made into transparencies to be used with an overhead projector. In this session, you will learn about the different types of charting formats available in Excel and how to create basic charts using worksheet information.

Before proceeding, make sure the following are true:

1. You have loaded Microsoft Windows and Excel.
2. You have an empty workbook displayed onscreen.
3. Your Advantage Diskette is inserted into the drive. You save your work onto the diskette and retrieve files that have been created for you.

FORMS OF BUSINESS GRAPHICS

Everybody has seen some sort of business graphic used at one time or another. From interest rates to unemployment statistics, most people prefer to see a picture of the latest trends than study the underlying numbers. There are several types of charts available for presenting information to different audiences such as engineers, statisticians, medical researchers, and business professionals. This section concentrates on the most popular business graphics, namely line charts, bar or column charts, pie charts, and XY or scatter plot diagrams.

LINE CHARTS

When you need to plot trends or show changes over a period of time, the **line chart** is the perfect tool. The angles of the line reflect variations in a trend, and the distance of the line from the horizontal axis represents the amount of the variation. An example of a line chart appears in Figure 5.1.

Figure 5.1

A line chart showing changes in television viewership over a five-year period

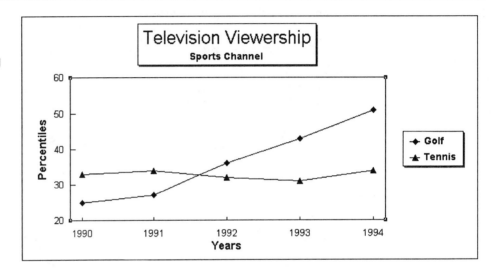

BAR OR COLUMN CHARTS

When the purpose of a chart is to compare one data element with another data element, a **column chart** is the appropriate form to use. A column chart also shows variations over a period of time, similarly to a line chart, and is one of the most commonly used graphs in business. An example appears in Figure 5.2. A *bar chart* also uses rectangular images, but they run horizontally rather than vertically.

Figure 5.2

A column chart comparing golf versus tennis viewership over a five-year period

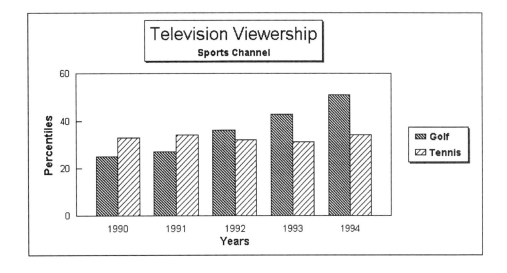

PIE CHARTS

A **pie chart** shows the proportions of individual components as compared to the total. Similar to a real pie (the baked variety), a pie chart is divided into slices. An example of a pie chart appears in Figure 5.3.

Figure 5.3

A pie chart showing the breakdown of expenses for XYZ Company

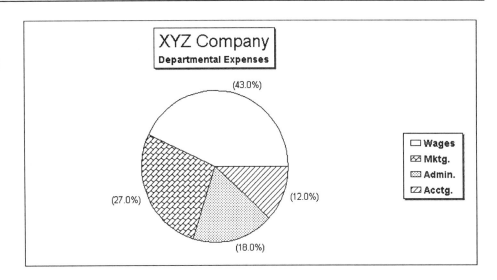

SCATTER PLOT CHARTS

XY charts, which are commonly referred to as *scatter plot diagrams*, show how one or more data elements relate to another data element.

Although they look much like line charts, XY charts include a numeric scale along both the X and Y axes. Figure 5.4 shows an XY chart.

Figure 5.4

An XY chart showing the correlation between worker stress and productivity

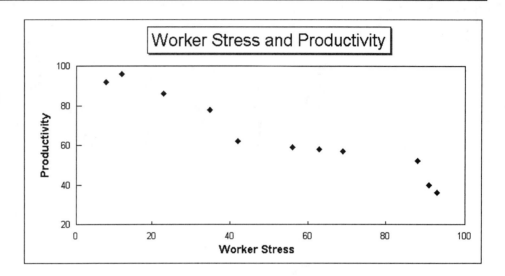

PRINCIPLES OF BUSINESS GRAPHICS

With graphics programs, there is often a tendency to overindulge in the various formatting and customizing options available. Although a picture may be worth a thousand words, it is probably wise not to test this adage with business graphics. Regardless of the sophistication of your graphics program, do not attempt to tell an entire history using a single chart. To assist your planning of when and how to apply business graphics, there are certain basic principles to follow: simplicity, unity, emphasis, and balance. The following sections describe each of these principles.

SIMPLICITY

One common problem with graphing is the tendency to put too much information and formatting onto a single chart. For example, using color to differentiate the slices of a pie chart works well. However, using different colors for a chart's title, background, **plot area** (the area for charting values), and legend is distracting. And although it is natural to want to tell the whole story in one chart, trying to do so may defeat its purpose. Charts are used to symbolize numbers or words because most people tend to find graphics easier to understand than straight text and tables. If you include too much text or detail in a chart, the visual aspects become muddled and the symbols become difficult to understand. Always try to keep your charts simple.

UNITY

A chart must clearly relate the data elements it contains—that is, it must appear as a unit. For instance, if you use too much space between the variables (such as between columns in a column chart), you will probably destroy the unity of your chart.

EMPHASIS

Use emphasis sparingly and correctly. Emphasis is used to draw one's attention to certain data elements or trends. For example, **exploding** a pie slice emphasizes that particular piece. In the same way, an arrow that points at a column in a column chart focuses the viewer's attention on that data element. Used correctly, formatting and customizing your chart to emphasize certain elements provide viewers with visual cues for focusing their attention.

BALANCE

Your graph should look balanced—both as a unit and in the context of the rest of the page. One factor that affects balance is the position of descriptive text, including titles, legends, and free-form text. Changing the position of such text affects the balance of the graph. Changing the shading, color, and thickness of the lines used in a graph also affects balance.

These four principles will assist you in developing charts that are easily read and interpreted. The next section introduces the methods for creating charts using Microsoft Excel. The concepts presented in this past section should be applied in the following sections.

USING EXCEL TO CREATE CHARTS

There are two methods for creating a chart in Excel, differing primarily in the way the chart is output and stored. First, you can create a new chart by selecting worksheet information and then choosing the Insert, Chart, As New Sheet command. This method adds a new chart sheet to the workbook and works well for creating computer-based presentations and slide shows. A second method allows you to create an **embedded chart** that you print and save along with the worksheet page. To create an embedded chart, select the worksheet information that you want plotted and then click the ChartWizard button (▒▒) or choose the Insert, Chart, On This Sheet command. Because an embedded chart resides directly on the worksheet, you can easily print the chart with its text and numbers. Regardless of the charting method you select, the **ChartWizard** guides you through the entire chart creation process using a series of dialog boxes.

Although Excel's default chart type is a column chart, there are many additional chart types available in Excel's gallery. Table 5.1 explains each type of chart.

	Chart Type	*Description*
Table 5.1		
Excel Chart Types	Area	Compares the amount of change in data elements over a period of time.
	Bar	Compares data elements over a period of time.
	Column	Compares data elements over a period of time.
	Line	Shows trends in data over a period of time.
	Pie	Shows the proportion of each individual element when compared to the total.
	Doughnut	Shows the proportion of each individual element when compared to the total; differs from pie chart in that you can display more than one data series.
	Radar	Shows each category as an axis or spoke from the center point.

Table 5.1 Continued	*Chart Type*	*Description*
	XY (Scatter plot)	Plots the relationships between different sets of data.
	3-D Area	3-D version of an area chart.
	3-D Bar	3-D version of a bar chart.
	3-D Column	3-D version of a column chart.
	3-D Line	3-D version of a line chart.
	3-D Pie	3-D version of a pie chart.
	3-D Surface	3-D version of a surface chart.

In the next section, you will create, print, and save a chart as a separate chart sheet in a workbook.

CREATING A CHART

You create a chart by selecting a range of cells to plot and issuing a menu command or clicking the ChartWizard button (▨). How does Excel know how to plot the information? What values does it place on the horizontal or **X-axis**? What values does it place on the vertical or **Y-axis**? Excel's decision process is examined in this section, along with the steps for creating a chart as a separate sheet in a workbook.

CHARTING A SINGLE RANGE

When you select a cell range to plot, Excel examines the shape of the highlighted area to determine what cells contain data and what cells contain headings or labels. If Excel finds text or dates in the left-hand column or in the top row, it then uses this information for the category and data labels. In other words, you should include the column headings and row labels when selecting a cell range so that Excel can automatically generate the labels for the X-axis and the legend.

In determining what information appears where, Excel counts the rows and columns in the selected range and plots the smaller dimension as the **data series** on the Y-axis. Excel always creates a chart based on the assumption that you want fewer data series than points along the X-axis. However, you can change this initial or default assumption in one of the dialog boxes (Step 4 of 5) displayed by the ChartWizard.

Perform the following steps to demonstrate the ChartWizard.

1. Ensure that you have an empty worksheet on the screen.

2. Create the worksheet appearing in Figure 5.5.

Figure 5.5

EMPLOYED
worksheet

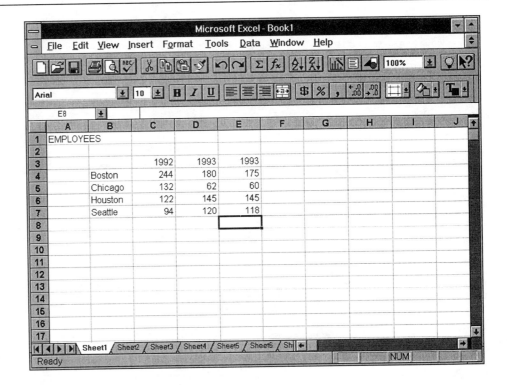

3. SELECT: cell range from B3 to E7
   Notice that there are more cities (4) than years (3) in this selection. Therefore, Excel will place the cities on the horizontal or X-axis and will plot the years on the vertical or Y-axis.

4. To plot the selected range as a new chart sheet in the workbook:
   CHOOSE: Insert, Chart, As New Sheet
   The ChartWizard displays the first dialog box in a series of five, as shown in Figure 5.6.

Figure 5.6

ChartWizard:
Step 1 of 5

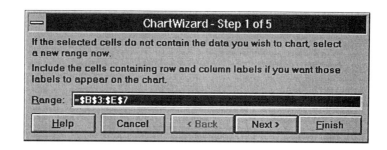

5. In the first dialog box, the ChartWizard confirms the cell range that you have selected. To accept this range as being accurate:
   SELECT: Next> command button
   The ChartWizard displays the second dialog box.

Figure 5.7

ChartWizard:
Step 2 of 5

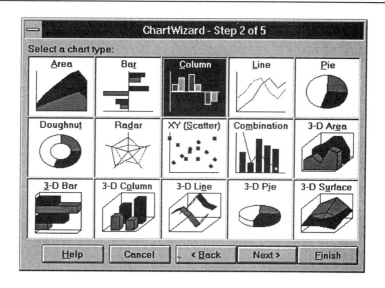

6. In Step 2 of 5, you select the type of chart that will best communicate your data (Figure 5.7). To proceed:
   SELECT: Next> command button
   The Step 3 dialog box (Figure 5.8) appears with alternative formats for the selected chart type.

Figure 5.8

ChartWizard:
Step 3 of 5

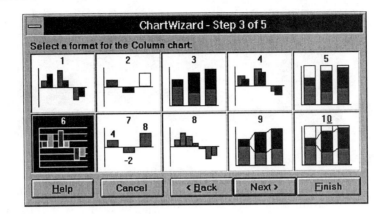

7. To accept the ChartWizard's default settings:
    SELECT: Next> command button
    The dialog box that appears is called Step 4 of 5.

Figure 5.9

ChartWizard:
Step 4 of 5

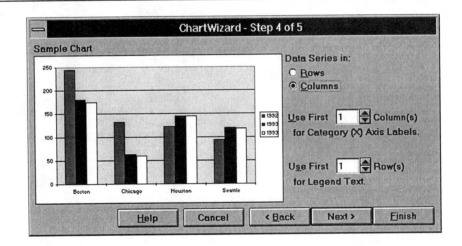

8. In this dialog box (Figure 5.9), you specify whether the column and
    row orientation is correct. In our example, the orientation is correct:
    CLICK: Next> command button

Figure 5.10

ChartWizard:
Step 5 of 5

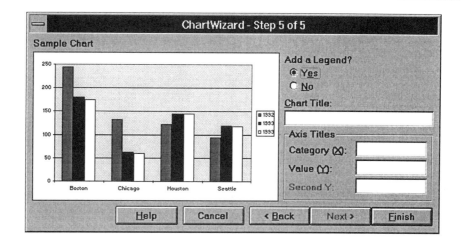

9. In the final dialog box (Figure 5.10), the ChartWizard lets you enter your own titles for the chart and axes as well as providing an option to turn the legend on and off. To proceed:
    CLICK: Finish command button
    The chart is displayed in a new sheet, called Chart1, in the same workbook file as the selected data.

10. To return to the worksheet:
    CLICK: Sheet1 tab

11. Let's demonstrate the link between the worksheet data and the chart:
    SELECT: cell C7
    TYPE: 300
    PRESS: (Enter)

12. To review the chart:
    CLICK: Chart1 tab
    Notice that the change in the worksheet data is immediately reflected in the chart sheet.

13. Save this workbook as EMPLOYED to the Advantage Diskette.

14. Close the workbook.

Quick Reference	1.	SELECT: the cell or range of cells to plot in a chart
Creating a Chart as	2.	CHOOSE: Insert, Chart, As New Sheet
a New Sheet	3.	Respond to the dialog boxes displayed by the ChartWizard.

CHARTING MULTIPLE RANGES

You can improve your productivity in Excel by reducing unnecessary keystrokes and commands. One method for reducing keystrokes is to select multiple cell ranges prior to formatting, deleting, or charting worksheet information. This allows you to place information anywhere in a workbook and still select it for charting. Because most worksheets are not as structurally perfect as the example in the last section, you must take advantage of this flexibility.

Perform the following steps to practice selecting multiple cell ranges for formatting and charting.

1. Open the XYZDEPT1 file located on the Advantage Diskette.

2. To format the GROSS RECEIPTS line, TOTAL EXPENSES line, and NET INCOME line to display a currency format, you must first select all the cell ranges:
   SELECT: cell range from B5 to E5

3. To select the range of cells from B13 to E13:
   PRESS: [Ctrl] and hold it down
   CLICK: cell B13 and hold down the mouse button
   DRAG: mouse pointer from B13 to E13
   Notice that the original cell selection of B5 to E5 remains highlighted.

4. Release the mouse button and the [Ctrl] key.

5. To select the range of cells from B15 to E15:
   PRESS: [Ctrl] and hold down
   CLICK: cell B15 and hold down the mouse button
   DRAG: mouse pointer from B15 to E15

6. Release the mouse button and the [Ctrl] key.

7. CLICK: Currency Style button ([$])
   Each of the highlighted cells is formatted to the currency format.

8. Let's select some ranges for charting. To highlight the cell range for the horizontal or X-axis:
   SELECT: cell range from A3 to D3
   (*Note*: Column E is not included because it is a summed value and we want to compare the months only.)

9. When selecting the data ranges to plot, you must ensure that they are the same shape (for example, same number of rows and columns) so that they will contain the same number of items:
   PRESS: Ctrl and hold it down
   SELECT: cell range from A5 to D5
   SELECT: cell range from A13 to D13

10. Release the Ctrl key.
    At this point, there should be three cell ranges selected on the worksheet as shown in Figure 5.11.

Figure 5.11

Selecting multiple ranges to chart

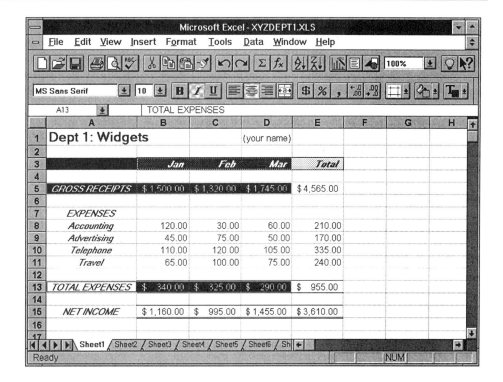

11. To produce a quick chart:
    CHOOSE: Insert, Chart, As New Sheet

12. When the first ChartWizard dialog box appears:
    SELECT: Finish command button
    A new chart sheet appears in the workbook. Notice that the Y-axis is formatted with dollar signs because of your earlier formatting of the GROSS RECEIPTS and TOTAL EXPENSES lines.

13. Let's rename the chart sheet's tab:
    DOUBLE-CLICK: Chart1 tab
    TYPE: Widgets
    PRESS: Enter

14. Save the workbook as XYZCHART onto the Advantage Diskette.

The next section explains some general features of charts. Do not close the chart or workbook as they are referred to in the following sections.

WORKING WITH CHARTS

When the chart sheet is active, Excel modifies your work area slightly. In addition to the appearance of the Chart toolbar, you will find additional menu commands specific to formatting and manipulating charts. Because chart sheets are quite different from worksheets, you may find that it takes some time to adjust. For example, you no longer have the familiar rows and columns to guide your entry of information. Before learning how to format and enhance charts in the next sections, take a few moments to study the parts of a chart labeled in Figure 5.12 and described in Table 5.2.

Figure 5.12

Parts of a Chart

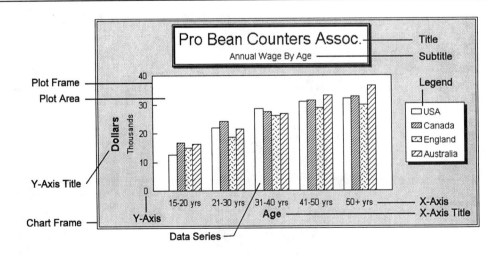

Table 5.2	Component	Description
Parts of a Chart Window	Chart and Chart Frame	The area inside a chart, including the plot area, titles, axes, legend, and other objects.
	Plot Area and Plot Frame	The area for plotting values from the worksheet. The plot area contains the axes and data series.
	Axes (X and Y) and Axes Titles	Most charts have a horizontal or X-axis and a vertical or Y-axis for plotting values.
	Data Marker	A single dot, bar, or symbol that represents one number from the worksheet.
	Data Series	A series of values from the worksheet that is related on the chart. A data series consists of related data markers.
	Legend	A key for deciphering the different data series appearing in the plot area.

In the next section, you learn how to select a chart type.

SELECTING A CHART TYPE

By default, Excel generates a column chart. However, there are many different chart types and formats to choose from in the gallery, as summarized in Table 5.1. This section shows you how to access these different chart formats.

Perform the following steps.

1. Ensure that the chart sheet is the active sheet:
   CLICK: Widgets tab

2. To select a different chart type:
   CHOOSE: Format, Chart Type
   The dialog box in Figure 5.13 appears.

Figure 5.13

Chart Type
dialog box

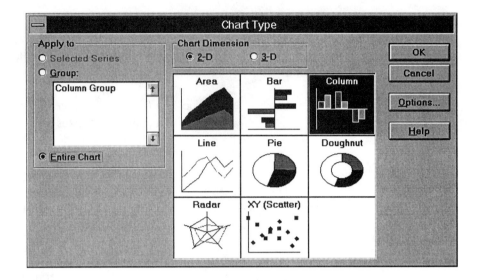

3. In the Chart Type dialog box:
   SELECT: 3-D option button under the Chart Dimension group
   SELECT: 3-D Bar option
   SELECT: Options command button
   The dialog box in Figure 5.14 appears.

Figure 5.14

Format 3-D Bar
Group dialog box

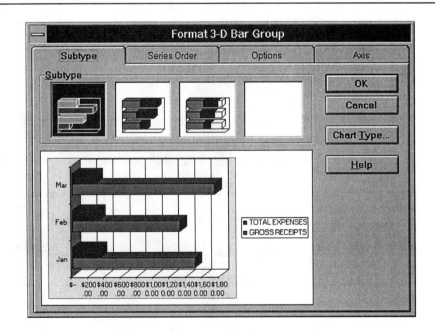

4. SELECT: leftmost (first) subtype
   PRESS: [Enter] or CLICK: OK

5. Practice changing the chart format using the Format, Chart Type command.

6. You can also apply predefined styles to your charts using the Format, AutoFormat command. There are two types of AutoFormat styles: Built-in (provided by Excel) and User-Defined (created by yourself). To demonstrate this powerful feature:
CHOOSE: Format, AutoFormat

7. In the dialog box that appears, make the following selections:
SELECT: Built-in option button under the Formats Used group
SELECT: 3-D Column from the Galleries list box
SELECT: 4 in the Formats grid area
PRESS: (Enter) or CLICK: OK
Your screen should now appear similar to Figure 5.15.

Figure 5.15

XYZCHART chart sheet

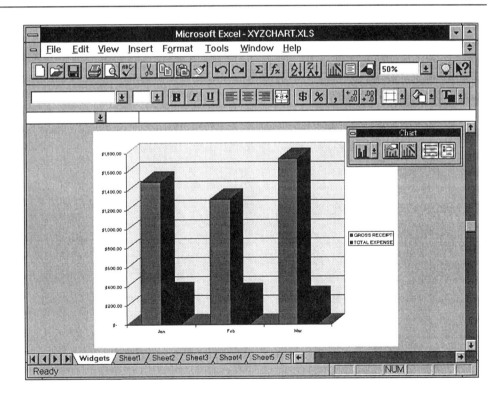

8. Save the workbook as XYZCHART to the Advantage Diskette, replacing the old version of the file.

Quick Reference	1. Make the chart sheet active.
Selecting a Chart	2. CHOOSE: Format, Chart Type
Type	3. In the dialog box, select the chart type.
	4. SELECT: Options command button
	5. In the dialog box, select the chart format.
	6. PRESS: [Enter] or CLICK: OK

CUSTOMIZING AND FORMATTING A CHART

Customizing a chart involves adding titles, legends, annotations, and arrows which emphasize certain aspects of the chart and improve its overall readability. Formatting a chart refers to setting the display options for each element of a chart. For example, if you are working on a color system, Excel differentiates each data series in a chart by assigning them different colors. When you print the chart to a non-color printer, however, the various colors appear as black or white. Therefore, you need to format the columns using patterns to differentiate the series. This section explores several methods for enhancing your chart.

To customize or format a chart, you must first select the chart item or object that you want to format. To select a single item using the mouse, simply click on the object. Using the keyboard, press the cursor-movement keys until the boxes appear around the object. The following sections demonstrate how to add titles, legends, free-form text, arrows, fonts, and patterns to your chart.

ATTACHING TITLES

Titles are used to state the purpose of the chart and to explain the scales used for the axes. After adding titles, you can format the text using a variety of fonts, styles, and shading. Perform the following steps to add a title to the WIDGETS graph.

1. Ensure that the chart sheet is active.

2. To add titles to the chart:
    CHOOSE: Insert, Titles
    SELECT: Chart Title check box
    SELECT: Value (Z) Axis check box
    SELECT: Category (X) Axis check box
    PRESS: [Enter] or CLICK: OK
    Excel places temporary text in each title location.

3. CLICK: Title once to select the object

4. Position the I-beam mouse pointer over the Title text and double-click
    to select the text.

5. To replace the title text:
    TYPE: Receipts vs. Expenses

6. To replace the X-axis title:
    CLICK: X-axis title once to select the object
    DOUBLE-CLICK: I-beam mouse pointer over the text in the axis
    TYPE: Months

7. To replace the Y-axis title:
    CLICK: Y-axis title once to select the object
    DOUBLE-CLICK: I-beam mouse pointer over the text in the axis
    TYPE: Dollars

Quick Reference	1. CHOOSE: Insert, Titles
Attaching Titles	2. SELECT: Chart Title, and the Value, Category, and Series Axes
	3. PRESS: [Enter] or CLICK: OK

ADDING A LEGEND

A **legend** provides a key for the data series plotted in the chart. If you
didn't specify a legend in the ChartWizard dialog box, you can add one
later using the Insert, Legend command. Excel places the legend at the
right-hand side of the chart window.

You can move the legend by dragging it using the mouse or by choosing a
command from its shortcut menu. Perform the following steps.

1. RIGHT-CLICK: *anywhere on the legend*
    CHOOSE: Format Legend from its shortcut menu

2. To change the legend's location on the chart sheet:
    CLICK: Placement tab
    The following options are available:

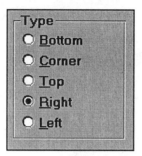

3. To move the legend to the top of the sheet:
    SELECT: Top option button
    PRESS: [Enter] or CLICK: OK

4. To move the legend to the bottom right-hand corner of the sheet, position the mouse pointer on the legend:
    CLICK: legend once and hold down the left mouse button
    DRAG: legend to the bottom right-hand corner

5. Release the mouse button.

6. To finalize the legend's position on the chart sheet:
    RIGHT-CLICK: *anywhere on the legend*
    CHOOSE: Format Legend
    CLICK: Placement tab
    SELECT: Right option button
    PRESS: [Enter] or CLICK: OK

Quick Reference
Adding a Legend
	• To add a legend to your chart:
	   CHOOSE: Insert, Legend
	• To format the legend:
	   RIGHT-CLICK: on the legend
	   CHOOSE: Format Legend

ENTERING FREE-FORM TEXT

With free-form text, you can easily emphasize important areas of a chart. Once text is entered, you can move it anywhere in the chart window and apply various fonts and styles.

Perform the following steps.

1. For the next two sections, we access buttons on the Drawing toolbar. To display the Drawing toolbar:
    RIGHT-CLICK: *on any button in the Standard or Formatting toolbars*
    CHOOSE: Drawing
    The Drawing toolbar should appear on your screen. Figure 5.16 labels the buttons on the Drawing toolbar.

Figure 5.16

Drawing toolbar

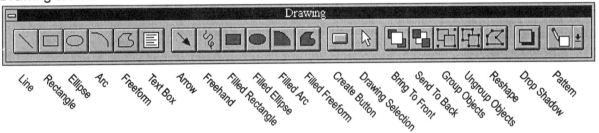

2. To provide a better view of your chart:
    CLICK: down arrow adjacent to the Zoom Control box (100%)
    SELECT: 100%

3. Scroll the window to view the upper-right quadrant of the chart.

4. To enter text, we will use the Text Box button on the Drawing toolbar:
    CLICK: Text Box button (▤)

5. Move the cross-hair mouse pointer into the chart sheet and drag a rectangle that is similar to the screen graphic in Figure 5.17.

Figure 5.17

Creating a text box

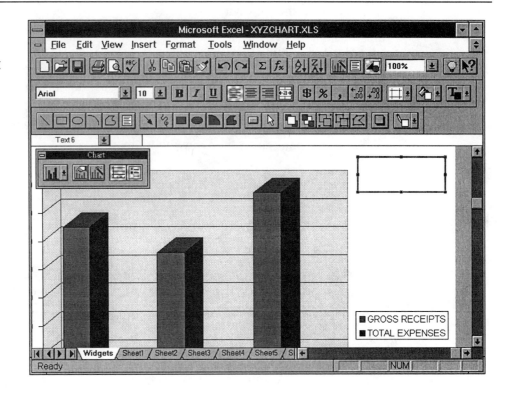

6. When you release the mouse button, you will notice a flashing insertion point. Do the following:
    TYPE: After Training

7. To remove the insertion point and deselect the text box:
    CLICK: on the white or gray area surrounding the chart

Quick Reference	1. CLICK: Text Box button (▤) on the Drawing toolbar
Adding Free-Form	2. DRAG: a rectangle in the chart sheet
Text	3. TYPE: any free-form text

USING ARROWS FOR EMPHASIS

Besides free-form text, you can use other types of objects to direct the reader's attention. Arrows are the most common means for focusing a viewer on certain locations in your chart. Perform the following steps.

1. To add an arrow to the chart:
    CLICK: Arrow button (◥) on the Drawing toolbar

2. Position the cross-hair mouse pointer below and to the left of the letter A in the word "After."

3. DRAG: the cross-hair mouse pointer towards the March GROSS RECEIPTS column (see below)

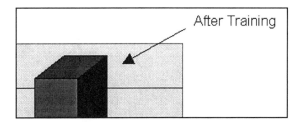

After Training

4. Release the mouse button. Your text box and arrow should appear similar to the above example.

Quick Reference	1. CLICK: Arrow button (⬊) on the Drawing toolbar
Adding an Arrow	2. DRAG: cross-hair mouse pointer in the chart sheet

CHOOSING FONTS AND PATTERNS

Formatting a chart involves changing its background color, choosing fonts for headings and other text, and selecting patterns for data series. In this section, you format the chart title and modify the columns in the plot area for printing on a noncolor printer. Although most commands are available in the Menu bar, you will find that the shortcut pop-up menus are much easier and more convenient to use for formatting a chart.

Perform the following steps.

1. To view the entire chart:
   CLICK: down arrow adjacent to the Zoom Control box (⎨100% ⎬)
   SELECT: 50%

2. Position the mouse pointer over the chart title and click the right mouse button to display its pop-up menu.

3. To enhance the text:
   CHOOSE: Format Chart Title
   CLICK: Font tab
   SELECT: Bold Italic from the Font Style list box
   SELECT: 18 point from the Size list box
   PRESS: (Enter) or CLICK: OK

4. RIGHT-CLICK: free-form text in the chart sheet

5. CHOOSE: Format Object
   CLICK: Font tab
   SELECT: Italic from the Font Style list box
   SELECT: 12 point from the Size list box
   PRESS: (Enter) or CLICK: OK

6. To display patterns, instead of colors, for the data series:
   RIGHT-CLICK: any one of the GROSS RECEIPTS columns

7. CHOOSE: Format Data Series
   CLICK: Patterns tab
   CLICK: down arrow adjacent to the Patterns drop-down list box
   SELECT: *an angled-line pattern*
   SELECT: black color
   PRESS: (Enter) or CLICK: OK

8. To display patterns for the TOTAL EXPENSES columns:
   RIGHT-CLICK: any one of the TOTAL EXPENSES columns
   CHOOSE: Format Data Series
   CLICK: Patterns tab
   CLICK: down arrow adjacent to the Patterns drop-down list box
   SELECT: *a shaded pattern*
   SELECT: black color
   PRESS: (Enter) or CLICK: OK

9. To format the legend box:
   RIGHT-CLICK: legend
   CHOOSE: Format Legend
   CLICK: Patterns tab
   SELECT: Shadow check box
   PRESS: (Enter) or CLICK: OK

10. Save the workbook as XYZCHART onto the Advantage Diskette, replacing the existing version of the chart. Your worksheet should now look similar to Figure 5.18.

Figure 5.18

A formatted and customized chart

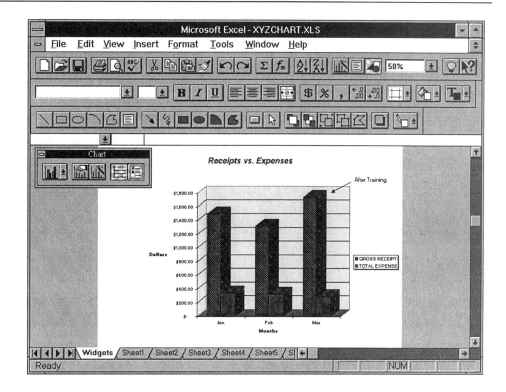

Quick Reference	1. RIGHT-CLICK: *a chart object*
Choosing Fonts	2. CHOOSE: Format *object command*
and Patterns	3. Complete the dialog box entries.
	4. PRESS: Enter or CLICK: OK

PRINTING A CHART

When a chart is created as a separate chart sheet, you print it directly from the chart sheet using the File, Print command. For the most part, the general print options are identical to printing a worksheet. However, there is one additional set of layout options for scaling the chart to fit on a page. Like a worksheet, you should always preview the chart prior to printing.

Perform the following steps to print the WIDGETS chart.

1. Ensure that the chart sheet is active.

2. To adjust the page layout options:
    CHOOSE: File, Page Setup
    CLICK: Chart tab
    The Page Setup dialog box appears as shown in Figure 5.19.

Figure 5.19

Page Setup dialog
box: Chart tab

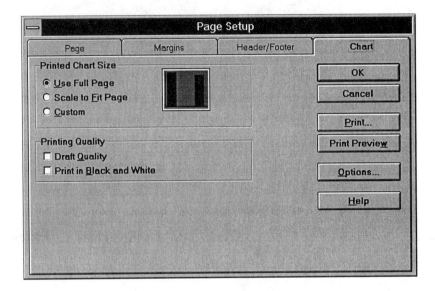

3. Select the appropriate size option for printing. The Scale to Fit Page option prints the chart using the current height to width ratio, and the Use Full Page option adjusts the ratio to maximize the print area. Try the following option on your printer:
    SELECT: Scale to Fit Page option button
    SELECT: Print Preview

4. When finished viewing the chart:
    PRESS: [Esc] or CLICK: Close

5. To send the chart to the printer:
    CHOOSE: File, Print
    PRESS: [Enter] or CLICK: OK

6. Save the workbook to the Advantage Diskette.

7. Close the workbook.

Quick Reference	1. Ensure that the chart sheet is active.
Printing a Chart	2. CHOOSE: File, Print
	3. Press (Enter) or click on OK

EMBEDDING A CHART

This section explains how to embed a chart into a worksheet using the ChartWizard. An embedded chart is placed over—not entered into—a cell range. All of the customizing and formatting for embedded charts is the same as for chart sheets. However, the methods for creating and printing the chart differ from previous sections.

To create an embedded chart, you select the cell range that you want to plot and then choose the Insert, Chart, On This Sheet command or click the ChartWizard button (📊). Either way, you must drag the cross-hair mouse pointer over an area on the worksheet to place the chart. Once the area is chosen, the ChartWizard leads you through a five-step process for formatting and customizing the chart. To remove an embedded chart, you select the chart by clicking on it and then press (Delete). To print worksheet information along with the chart, you select a range that covers both areas of the worksheet and chart, set the desired page layout options, and then choose the File, Print command. To edit an embedded chart, you simply double-click the chart to make it active.

Perform the following steps.

1.   Open the CRUISES worksheet located on the Advantage Diskette.

2.   SELECT: cell range from A2 to D5

3.   To use the ChartWizard:
     CLICK: ChartWizard button (📊)
     (*Hint*: You should always look in the Status bar for helpful messages. For example, "Drag in document to create a chart" now appears.)

4.   To place the embedded chart below the worksheet information, first move the cross-hair mouse pointer to the middle of cell A7.

5. CLICK: cell A7 and hold down the mouse button
   DRAG: cell A7 to D15
   The borderlines extend as you drag the mouse to D15. To make a perfect square, you hold down the (**Shift**) key as you drag the mouse. To align the chart with worksheet cells, you hold down the (**Alt**) key.

6. Release the mouse button.

7. The ChartWizard takes over and displays the first of five dialog boxes for confirming the cell range to plot. Since you selected the cell range before accessing the ChartWizard, the range is correct. To proceed:
   CLICK: Next> command button

8. In the second dialog box, you specify the type of chart:
   SELECT: Column chart
   CLICK: Next> command button
   (*Note*: At any time, you can click the <Back command button to return to a previous step.)

9. In the third dialog box, you select the format for the chosen chart type:
   SELECT: option 3 for a stacked column chart
   CLICK: Next> command button

10. In the fourth dialog box, you confirm the layout of the cell range and the appearance of the Sample Chart. To proceed to the next step:
    CLICK: Next> command button

11. In the fifth and last dialog box, you specify whether you want a legend and enter the titles for the chart and axes. Do the following:
    SELECT: Yes for Add a legend?
    CLICK: the Chart Title text box
    TYPE: `Demographics`
    CLICK: the Value (Y) text box
    TYPE: `Passengers`
    Notice that the information that you typed for the titles is immediately placed into the Sample Chart window.

12. To finish using the ChartWizard:
    PRESS: (**Enter**) or CLICK: Finish
    The chart appears on the worksheet.

13. To move the chart, first select the chart by clicking in the middle of it and then drag it to a new location:
CLICK: embedded chart once and hold down the mouse button
DRAG: chart back and forth to finalize its position

14. To size the chart, first select the chart and then position the mouse pointer over one of the boxes on the embedded chart's borderlines. The mouse pointer should change to a cross hair.

15. CLICK: once and hold down the mouse button
DRAG: borderline back and forth to finalize the size
Size the chart to match the worksheet screen in Figure 5.20.

Figure 5.20

Manipulating an embedded chart

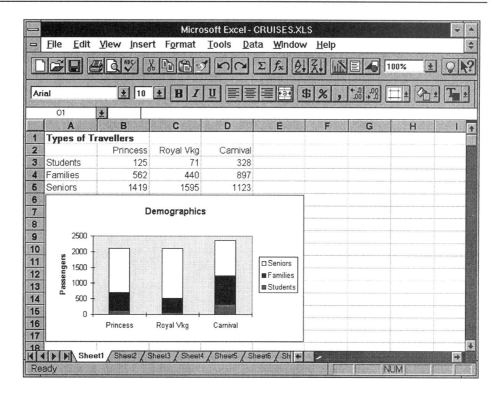

16. To print the worksheet:
SELECT: *the entire cell range from A1 to the bottom right-hand corner of the embedded chart*
CHOOSE: File, Print
PRESS: Enter or CLICK: OK

17. Save the worksheet to the Advantage Diskette and exit Excel.

Quick Reference	1. Select the cell range or ranges to include in the chart.
Creating an	2. CLICK: ChartWizard button (📊) on the toolbar
Embedded Chart	3. CLICK: cell where you want to place the top left corner of the chart and hold the left mouse button down
Using the	4. DRAG: the mouse pointer to the cell where you want to put the bottom right corner of the chart
ChartWizard	5. Release the mouse button.
	6. Proceed through the five dialog boxes making selections for your chart and pressing the Next> command button. In the fifth dialog box, click the Finish command button to finalize the chart.

SUMMARY

This session discussed the benefits of using graphics to present worksheet information. Besides introducing several types of business graphics, the basic principles of graphing, including simplicity, unity, emphasis, and balance, were explained. In Excel, there are two methods for creating charts from worksheet information. A chart can be created, printed, and saved as a separate sheet in a workbook or embedded into an existing worksheet. In this session, you practiced both methods for creating a chart, including using the ChartWizard's step-by-step approach.

Excel provides several customizing and formatting options for enhancing a chart, including fonts, patterns, titles, legends, and annotations. With approximately 90 different charting formats, it is guaranteed you will find the perfect tool to help you make that winning presentation! Table 5.3 summarizes the commands introduced in this session.

Table 5.3	*Command*	*Description*
Command Summary	Insert, Chart, As New Sheet	Creates a chart in a separate sheet of the current workbook file.
	Insert, Chart, On This Sheet	Creates an embedded chart on the current worksheet from the highlighted range.
	Format, Chart Type	Selects the type and format of chart to display.
	Format, AutoFormat	Selects and applies a predefined style to a chart.

	Command	Description
Table 5.3 Continued	Insert, Titles	Adds titles for the chart and X- and Y-axis.
	Insert, Legend	Adds a legend to the chart.

KEY TERMS

ChartWizard   A collection of dialog boxes that leads you through creating an embedded chart on a worksheet.

column chart   A chart that compares one data element with another data element and can show variations over a period of time.

data series   A series of values from the worksheet that are related.

embedded chart   An Excel chart that is placed over worksheet cells and printed and saved along with the worksheet file.

exploding   Refers to a slice in a pie chart that is partially removed from the rest of the pie for emphasis.

graphics   The pictorial representation of words and data.

legend   A key for deciphering the data series appearing in the plot area of a chart.

line chart   A chart that plots trends or shows changes over a period of time.

pie chart   A chart that shows the proportions of individual components as compared to the whole.

plot area   The area for plotting values from the worksheet. The plot area contains the axes and data series.

X-axis   The horizontal axis that shows the categories for which the chart is making comparisons.

XY charts   Charts that show how one or more data elements relate to another data element. Also called *scatter plot diagrams*.

Y-axis   The vertical axis that shows the value or measurement unit for making comparisons among the various categories.

EXERCISES

SHORT ANSWER

1. Describe the basic principles of using graphics.
2. Describe the process of creating a chart as a separate sheet.
3. Describe the process of creating an embedded chart.
4. How do you move an embedded chart using the mouse?
5. List the different types of charts found in the Chart Type dialog box.
6. What are some options for moving the legend around the screen?
7. Describe the process of adding a text box to a chart.
8. Describe the process of adding an arrow to a chart.
9. How are chart objects selected using the keyboard?
10. How do you make an embedded chart active and ready for editing?

HANDS-ON

(*Note*: In the following exercises, save your workbooks onto and retrieve files from the Advantage Diskette.)

1. The objective of this exercise is to create a worksheet and an embedded pie chart that show the breakdown of your total monthly expenses:
    a. Ensure that you have an empty workbook.
    b. Enter your name in cell A1.
    c. Create a worksheet that lists the following expense headings on separate rows within a single column: RENT, FOOD, GAS, and FUN.
    d. Enter your monthly expense amounts in the column to the right of the row headings. (You can enter any values, not necessarily your own.)
    e. Select the row headings and values to produce an embedded chart.
    f. CLICK: ChartWizard button (📊)

g. Place the chart to the right of the present worksheet information and size it to cover fifteen rows by five columns.

h. Following the steps for each dialog box, select a 3-D pie chart that displays the names beside each pie wedge. Add a title to the chart that has the words "Monthly Expenses" on the first line.

i. Once the chart appears on the worksheet:
DOUBLE-CLICK: embedded chart to make it active

j. Select different patterns for the pie wedges for printing on a black-and-white laser or dot matrix printer.

k. Print the worksheet and chart on the same page.

l. Save the workbook as MYEXP onto the Advantage Diskette.

2. In this exercise you retrieve a workbook and then create a line chart, stacked column chart, and a 3-D column chart.

a. Close all of the open windows in the document area.

b. Open the CHARTS workbook located on the Advantage Diskette. This worksheet is a planning tool used by XYZ Company to project sales and production. (Make sure to type your name into cell A3.)

c. Create one line chart, in a separate chart sheet, showing the number of units sold for each product over the five-year period.

d. Add an appropriate title to the chart.

e. Name the sheet's tab LINE.

f. Print the chart using the Scale to Fit Page option.

g. Create one stacked column chart, in a separate chart sheet, that displays the revenue for each product over the five-year period. A stacked chart displays each product's portion of the total revenue in a single column for each year.

h. Add an appropriate title to the chart.

i. Name the sheet's tab STACK.

j. Print the chart using the Use Full Page option.

k. Create one 3-D column chart, in a separate chart sheet, to compare the Total Revenue versus the Total Costs over the five-year period.

l. Add an appropriate title to the chart.

m. Name the sheet's tab COLUMN.

n. Print the chart using the Scale to Fit Page option.

o. Save the workbook as CHARTING onto the Advantage Diskette.

p. Close all of the open windows in the document area.

q. Exit Excel.

r. Exit Windows.

INDEX

MICROSOFT EXCEL 5.0

present value, 104, 107, 115
Print Manager, 72, 82
print queue, 73, 82
printing a chart, 187
printing a workbook, 72, 79
   defining the page layout, 73
   previewing the output, 78
Program Manager, 10, 40

range name, 101, 115
relative cell address, 89, 115
rounded value, 109, 115
row height, 56, 82

saving and closing a workbook,
   34

scatter plot diagram, 165
series, 96, 115
Sheet tabs, 14, 136
shortcut menus, 16
Solver, 110, 115
Spell Checker, 49
splitting the document window,
   128
Standard toolbar, 13, 19
starting Excel, 10
SUM function, 51, 82
Summary Info dialog box, 36

TipWizard, 23
typefaces, 59, 82

Undo command, 34, 40

vertical split box, 128, 155
Visual Basic, 148

what-if analysis, 4, 40, 110
workbook, 7, 13, 15, 40
WYSIWYG, 6, 40

X-axis, 169, 193
XY chart, 165, 194

Y-axis, 169, 194